Autobiography of a Yogini

A Black Woman's Love Affair with her Guru

Autobiography of a Yogini

A Black Woman's Love Affair with her Guru

Kamala Easton, Ph.D.

Embodying the Goddess Book Publishing
Sante Fe, New Mexico

Autobiography of a Yogini
A Black Woman's Love Affair with her Guru
Published by
Embodying the Goddess Book Publishing
903 W. Alameda St. #208
Santa Fe, NM 87501
(505) 983-0108
kamalaeaston@gmail.com

Kamala Easton, Publisher
Quality Press, Production Coordinator
BlackWorks, Interior and Cover Layout

Embodying the Goddess Books are available at special discounts
for bulk purchases, sales promotions, fundraising or educational
purposes.

Copyright © 2012 by Kamala Easton
ISBN #: 978-0-615-70862-1
Library of Congress Control Number: 2012950820

DEDICATION

This book is dedicated to my wonderful daughter Krystal, whose joy in my life has been the greatest, and who has stood by me in love, no matter our differences in spirituality. I Love You and I pray that this book brings riches to your life.

And to the Guru (both within and without), for carrying the vibration that changed my life and my heart.

ACKNOWLEDGEMENTS

I would like to acknowledge the help of two individuals who lovingly and kindly read this manuscript and shared with me their heart's ideas doing their best to be gentle when questions arose; Darlene Kennedy and Ann Schmidt. Thank you for your time and your consideration.

Suzie Arnett who helped me to get moving when I had been stuck for a long time, thank you for your encouragement.

Courtney (CC Skye) for remembering our goddess connection, and taking the time out of your busy schedule to read and share your ideas and helping me with some important details.

Jessica Grace and Gisela Stromeyer for your help and support.

CONTENTS

Prologue

This is a book about love, longing and transformation. Loving, longing and transforming relationship to self. Love, longing and transforming relationship to a man. But mostly, this book is about my deep and abiding trust and transformation of my relationship with this thing that most do not understand - Spirit or God. This thing that we cannot see or measure or know with certainty. This thing that we either believe to be true or not. That we pray will assist us in our times of need. And yet most of us long to prove Its existence. Either thru an unwavering belief, or through experiences which help us to *know*, but for some, there is becoming the actual desire to *know* on an even deeper level, to actually *experience* it – first hand: the actual allowing of It to become merged with who we are. So that we can become the individuals on this planet that we were meant to be: women and men filled with the substance of the Divine.

A prologue is usually something that is used as an introduction to fiction. Much of what you will read may be thought by many to, in fact, be fiction. The experiences I have had are extraordinary, which even at the time in which they were occurring, a part of my mind was consciously viewing and aware of their inconceivable and otherworldliness. I had in fact, no way of comprehending or believing much of what occurred, except by the fact that I was experiencing them. Given that I had been in the academic research world (see it/analyze it to believe it) for many many years, I knew that my perceptions were from a grounded real-world place, and yet they were still 'beyond belief'.

This is a book about my life. Most of what is included occurred over a 7-year period. But it is the substance of who I now am. I am a woman who has merged with the Divine. I am one with the All. I have come to this state of being thru my struggles with self-transformation and especially with one Holy Man – Sri Sri Ravi Shankar, spiritual leader of the International Art of Living Foundation. His programs spread across 150 countries and have over 20 million followers. He has met with Presidents and dignitaries from almost every country on earth, including George W. Bush, and recently received an accommodation from Vice President Joe Biden. This powerful spiritual world leader, however, is also a man. Unlike many gurus in the east, he does not wear ochre colored robes; he wears white leaving his desire for human love and marriage, open for discussion. His magnetism and charm is so well-known in India, that many famous men and women there have steered clear of him as to not be taken over by his power.

Because of my early aversion to gurus, I did not immediately fall for him. I was simply filled with gratitude towards him, for the positive changes, which had happened in my life as a result of taking his courses. But eventually, he turned his powers towards me and I, like so many other Westerners, 'fell in love with my guru'. He is the man who transformed me. He is the man who filled my heart with love; he is the man who helped me to become happy. He is the man who helped me to answer my question: "What would life be like if this, that I have come to know as Spirit, ruled every moment?"

There is no way for those in the West to understand the power of the guru. How a being could use other people to "speak thru them" to another, as in our first meeting where he picked up a man who I had never met, at the end of a week-long course, brought him clear across the room, and had him whisper words of love in my ear. Or how years later, as I sat down next to a woman whom I barely knew in a Satsang of 500, she began saying to me "When you walk into a room, it is as if no one else exists", and immediately she said, "I have no idea why I am saying this." My experiences with him and with India made me see Western spirituality similar to the saying: "If you grow up in a cave, you don't know the sun exists." Such is true of our limited understanding of Spirit. In India, the roof came off of my spiritual knowing and understanding, and especially through knowing this man. And, because I already had a deep deep love of the Divine, his magnetic powers, merging with the love in my heart for the "Divine Only", created an internal explosion of godliness within myself. I was very much like Mira the Indian mystic or St. Theresa of Avila or Guru Nanak, overwhelmed by the intimate love of God.

> *In India when sitting in a Satsang (a gathering of people, singing, praying and meditating) with the guru on the stage my eyes were closed and I was deep in meditation. In the midst of the music and joy, a vision of my left breast rose in my mind's eye directly in front of me. I opened my eyes and came out of my deep state as I was startled because I rarely and still to this day, "see" things. I settled down, re-closed my eyes and began to go back into my meditation, when the vision appeared again. This time, however, there was a stream of water pouring forth from it. Simultaneously, I felt my Third Eye, the area between my eyebrows, energetically open up and energy began to pour forth from it like a giant fire hose. The energy poured directly up towards the stage and onto the guru. I opened my eyes enough to see him affected by it. I closed them loosely and began to sway my body and head with the rhythm of the music, and as I swayed, his body on the stage moved to the same rhythmic pattern as if energetically held and controlled by each movement of my body.*

Some of what you will read will be from my own perceptions, as well as my latent understandings (partly because of my inexperience and resulting ignorance of the male mind, and much because of my inability to perceive the subtleness of Indian and Guru Cultures in which I became immersed.) You will see me from my limited perspective of a "Westerner" in an Eastern world, trying to fill in the gaps from after-the-fact insights and revelations from others. Therefore, my conclusions are often very late and possibly incorrect. But the facts, which occurred, did. And I am a much better being because of them.

I also share my story because there is too little written about the "How To's" of transformation. We have only a few examples available to us of how the realization of our Higher Self's (or at least becoming better beings) that most of us, if only on a subconscious level, pray we will become, can occur and that it can, in fact exist. It is the story of my spiritual transformation. We in the West do not know how people become one with the All. We believe that Christ did/was. But, we have no idea of *how* he became who He was. There are a few stories of saints, mystics, Buddha, Krishna, or we have read that there are certain steps or paths to the Divine but not enough for us to understand that everyone's process is different, that there is no ABC formula, that we didn't have to have out-of-body experiences or see visions of angels or Buddha as a young child. We need to know that ordinary human beings, living out our day-to-day problems, loving, fearing, existing can in fact merge into the Oneness. Whoever we are, however we choose to express it, we can each become the expression of the Divine Spirit in Man/Woman.

As stated by the great teacher of the West "greater things than this shall ye do." We should be able to begin this journey some 2000 years after His passing. We are here to do this. Each of us in our unique expression will come to the point at some time on our soul's journey, of merging with the All and sharing our Divine Self through this uniqueness. This is simply my story.

INTRODUCTION

God Seduced Me - Showering me with earthly riches that I could never have dreamt of, It slowly, yet profoundly grabbed my EVERYTHING.

Growing up as a young black teenager in the 60's I had negative preconceptions of Gurus and Hinduism. In high school I can remember seeing Rajneesh and his Rolls Royces on TV and with my girlfriends laughing and saying, "That's just a bunch of crazy white folks following gurus." Later, while attending UC Berkeley, I can remember being stunned on the first day and bothered every day thereafter, when in order to walk onto campus I had to pace past the Hari Krishnas in their strange orange garb, shaved heads and painted faces dancing and singing at me.

I had re-remembered Its existence from my childhood days of Catholicism, in which I had completely released It after Vatican II when I returned from a summer at my grandparents' and found my priests married to my nuns and pregnant.. That first "remembrance", some 15 years before, came when I was in dire straits during some not very proud moments of Black disco life in 70's Manhattan. He/It made me know that It existed by saving me from those very fast days and beginning my journey first in natural health, vegetarianism, positive thinking, affirmations, and meditation. As the years went by, while still living a very academic and hard working administrative life, I began to read everything Western Spirituality had to offer, Theosophists, Jungian, High level Christ Based Thought, trying to understand my own self and the Divine. But never from the place of: "How can I become that?" or "What is God?" I always felt that that was too big of a question to even be interested in attempting to understand, simply more about how this thing that was beyond my comprehension might help me in living the best life that I could live NOW.

But after years of trying, I was still smothered with personal pain and grief – in my inability to be in relationship with a man, which even the deep deep love and bond with my child did not assuage.

I had been raised by a single black mother, with no men around; and as a result, I knew nothing about being with them. I never knew how to speak softly to them, never knew what their needs were, never knew how to ask for help and never knew how to let them come to me. All things that, in my later adult life, I learned were quintessential in interactions between men and women.

However, as a young woman growing up without these ways of knowing and being, and seeing my mother do-it-all, I remember in my early 20's consciously and honestly asking the question "What do you need a man for?"

It was this internal contradiction: not knowing what a man was for and at the same time the longing to have a mate, that thing which *everyone* had, that predicated my relations with men.

However, by the time I was a single Mother myself, I began to see the answers to the question; because by then, I realized how wonderful it would be to have someone else contributing to the income, someone else to share the needs of my child, someone else to protect me, someone to care for me, and someone to love. But at the time, I didn't understand these needs, nor was I able to fulfill them.

So with all that pain, I turned to the earth and cried my heart out into the trees and hills and valleys, anywhere It/Nature could hear me, feel me. I cried so hard over my loneliness, until one day after a week in Kauai where I had hiked up into the jungle and dumped my All into the roots of a powerful tree, I returned and had a dream of The Tree of Life, lifted out of the earth, huge, almost a city block in diameter, roots hanging from the sky above me, revealing its power and majesty to me; letting me know that She/He had heard my call.

At the same time, God was seducing me with these worldly riches – a beautiful home in Topanga Canyon, natural and lovely complete with indoor sauna, endless views of Nature, and magnificent mountainous hikes right out my back door. In those hills, it began to show me my power, the power of my tears, breaking through the heartache into manifestation.

Next it was on to the luxury of Malibu – the most beautiful home that any of my wealthiest friends had ever seen. Twenty acres, a 40 ft master bedroom with views of both the ocean and pristine canyons and a bathroom with a three-step sunken tub and equal views, which was so grand that once when having a party I found a girlfriend's visiting relative standing inside it taking pictures cause "honey we don't have anything like this in Jersey!" All of these things gifted to me by the Divine, as I was still a financially struggling Single Mom.

It was through these riches that – God Grabbed Me. God made me WANT Him/Her. Want to know IT, Fully – completely. Soon the day came when I asked the question of my life – "What would it be like if I allowed this thing that I had come to know intimately as Spirit – what would life be like if I allowed IT to make EVERY decision in my life?" In other words, what if my Ph.D./Do-it-all/Know-it-all mind, no longer ran the show. No longer made the choices, no longer solved the day-to-day problems and issues of life. What would life be like if I turned it ALL over?????

Perhaps I imagined that there would be more Malibu Mansions, no more problems, smooth sailing. But I don't really remember thinking that. I just wanted to know what it would be like: What life would be like with God in charge? In my heart of hearts, I believed that we did not have to DO to BE, that the birds and the animals are put here on this planet to live a perfect bird/animal life. And they do, so why not man/woman? Why do we have to struggle so to survive on this earth? It made no sense to me. But I had never known or seen or even heard of anything else. Even though The Divine had intervened and brought me to one of the wealthiest of environments in the country, as a single Mom, I was still very much struggling financially and emotionally.

My mother had done her best, but with much limitation. I had *chosen* a very angry single black woman who had to "pitch pennies" in order to give me the best that she could and to see to it that I received a good education. But, because she was filled with harsh perfectionist expectations and so much internal pain herself, I got hurt: whipped and belittled, whenever I could not live up to them. The resulting levels of fear, pain and internal scarring created a life of struggle and inability to stand FOR myself or to say NO to abuse, which I now know; I came here to *move through.*

As I was in the process of completing my doctorate and with 20 years of higher education experience behind me, I knew that the next "J O B" /"Position" would have me forever, i.e, Vice-President of this, Dean of that, I knew that. NOW was the perfect time for me to see this question out. And so, without any thought of the consequences to myself, my child or my life------ I stepped out into the unknown. I did it by allowing each bill, each problem, everything to be handled by Spirit (or at least not handled by me). I had left my research job at the university when I finished my doctorate, and so I had no income. And yet, of course the bills kept coming. And in those moments, I chose to be STILL, to see what would happen if I didn't try to figure out a way to pay/solve them. I stood still and trembled as each approaching bill's due date came closer and closer. What I found was, in the end, it passed, I was still standing (even with a whew!), and I began to see one by one, that life would continue, albeit different, but that those things that run our lives, those things that push us to struggle, are in fact not real. There is a reality beneath them, on which one could live without the struggle and strife.

> *Later I realized that there could have been a way to REQUEST that all be handled in a smooth and easy way, as we are in fact co-creators with the Divine. But at that time all I knew to do was surrender.*

I remember I had a dream about that time, where everyone who lived at this Malibu compound had to run to the highest point above the land as a Tidal Wave was coming and it was going to kill us all. We stood in a group overlooking the ocean. And I knew that someone would have to be sacrificed in order to save us all. And, without a thought, the young woman present, jumped off the cliff, into the approaching water.

From that day on, Life was never the same.

Chapter 1

I love you, I love you, I love you, I love you – First Meeting

I never wanted him. I had an aversion to gurus. One day when I could no longer take it, I exploded at one of my housemates whose room was filled with photos of a multitude of gurus. I asked her "Why do you *need* all these gurus!? Don't you have your own direct connection to God?!"

However, because my Ph.D. program was causing me so much stress, I ended up taking a master's program in movement therapy in order to connect with my body and to try to get out of my head. (I also led a women's full moon hiking group in the canyon where I lived and wanted to incorporate movement with our group.) In the program, I studied among other things the works of Alexander Lowen, founder of Bio-Energetics. He taught that all of the traumas of our lives were stored in our bodies. Anger, in which we grit our teeth and clinch our fists, often leads to TMJ in the jaws and arthritis in the hands. Fear, he said, was the posture of tightening our shoulders and lower back (or tails) tucked in, often resulting in neck tension and lower back pain. He gave exercises to help release this stress from within and I found them extremely useful. As I read more of his work, he began to talk about the importance of the breath, and how we could use the breath to release stress that was even more deeply lodged in our cells. He created a series of breath therapies and trained psychologists to work with patients using these techniques. I signed up with one who lived near me in Topanga Canyon, and had a session. It was fine, but just fine. A few days later, I opened up the "L.A. Weekly" paper and saw an advertisement for "The Healing Breath Workshop" with a picture of the one male guru who that same housemate had recently gone to see. I decided to take the course as I had had enough of being in my head, and even though I wasn't really interested in being connected with a guru, I decided that I would rather have a *spiritual* breath course than a *psychological* one.

The course was immediately transformative. In that first weekend course, I cried so hard as I released and yet the interesting thing was that I had no memories associated with it. Just a powerful letting go of emotions that felt as if they had been stored for a lifetime. For the next six months I did the breath work daily as well as attended weekly Satsangs, in which as a group, we did a longer more intense version and afterwards they chanted and ate together. However, I left as soon as they began the chants, as I didn't want anything to do with that, regardless; the course changed my life significantly. The previous six years in my doctoral program had felt like someone was pulling my back teeth, but after taking the course, my dissertation literally flew out of my fingertips, and somewhere in that time I realized that I was "happy". I didn't know that I was "not happy" before that, but all of a sudden I was. I was lighter, more energetic and feeling that I could take on the world. I was ready to teach this yogic course to the world, as I was a natural born teacher.

Soon the guru who created the course was coming to Los Angeles. There was to be an advanced course with him present and a talk the evening before at a local church that I had been connected with over some time, in fact I personally knew the minister. And so, I went to the evening event to see Him for the first time. I don't remember much, except that he made the minister feel that he had spoken too much, by choosing not to speak himself after the minister was finished. He simply decided to lead a prayer, as the minister apologized profusely. During the event, I sat next to a woman from that church. We had a very personal conversation, and I shared with her that I had difficulties in relationships. At the end of the prayer, everyone was invited up to hug the guru. After the procession was near completion, that woman had gone up and hugged him and returned to her seat. She asked me did I go up or how was it for me? I said, "No, I didn't go to him." She turned to me, looked me in the eye and said, "That's your problem with men, you better go up there and get some of that man's loving!"….. But I didn't.

Later, at the very end of the program, on my way out, I did go up to the podium, but I stopped and spoke only to my minister friend never acknowledging the being in the white robes standing just beside him, even though I was registered to take his weeklong course beginning the very next day. I think something inside of me just told me to stay away.

The very next morning the course began. Three hundred or so of us piled up to Malibu at a retreat center and as I lived in Malibu, I did not stay on site, but drove up every day. It was nothing fancy; I think it was a Jewish summer camp. I went to the registration table and saw a woman who I knew. After a little confusion about the change in my last name, I registered and settled into my spot with backjack, pillows and blankets to get ready for a week of I knew not what. But, it was exciting; the room was full of people and energy. The weeklong course was held in silence, which for me was unique as I had gone to many spiritual courses and retreats before, but I don't remember being in continued silence. Because we could not speak, the course leaders had what they called a Question Basket – for us to place (anonymously) any questions we had regarding how the course was handled and/or general inquiries. These questions were read out loud and answered. There was also what was called a "Botheration" Basket. At first I wasn't sure what this was for, except that we were to place any/all problems and complaints (also anonymously), things that were keeping us from enjoying the course or internal or external issues that we just had problems with. These issues were not read aloud, and much later I assumed it was there for us to release from our minds and hearts anything that would keep us from fully participating in the program.

I can say that I was enjoying the course overall, in that I found the guru to be kind, loving, knowledgeable and fun. At one point he even shocked the entire group by pulling out a large water gun from under his seat and squirting most of the crowd, who raised their hands to be the lucky ones to receive his shower. However, I was not happy seeing the way in which the participants treated the guru; all the bowing down and following him around, it made me want to throw up. And so, I chose to write it out, on the "botheration" slip.

Well, to my surprise, one evening, as the guru was reading some of the notes from the, "Question and Answer" basket himself, I heard him speak the words from one of my "Botherations" ... "Why is it that all these people follow you around and bow down to you and put all those flowers around you, etc. etc. etc......?! Aren't you just there to be a reflection of what we are supposed to be, of our highest?????!!!!!" I was shocked to hear the words (which were only supposed to be contained in that "other" basket) come out of his mouth. And, by the immediate stillness in the room, so was everyone else. He paused, and then smiled and finally responded by saying that from his perspective up on the stage, he could not see the flowers and that we in the audience were the ones who could see them, so, they were in fact for us. He gently laughed it off and made the crowd laugh, which did lighten the moment. However, the very next day, he more perfectly answered my question.

We were coming back from our afternoon break and only half of the audience had taken their places when he walked in on the side right in front of where I was sitting, and for the first time, he was by himself, no entourage. He tiptoed in over people and when they saw him, and they got ready to quickly stand up and bow down, he gestured with his hand to, "No, stay seated." And then he quietly walked up onto the stage. He let me know right off that those things that concerned me, were not, in actuality, required.

A few days later, my second and most embarrassing botheration was read aloud, especially because it almost pinpointed me and caused the woman sitting next to me, whom I alluded to in the note, to become obvious. Even though my words showed a beautiful reconciliation of the conflict within myself, the lessons were great, hopefully, for both of us.

At some point we were told that anyone who wanted to could have a personal meeting with him as part of a small group. Of course I did, and waited for my day. We stood outside of his house, but things were greatly delayed, and we were the last group for the afternoon. When we finally did go in, it was only for five minutes or so. We barely got to spend any time with him. I was quite upset, as it did not seem fair that we had waited so long and got cut short because the previous groups had taken so long. Soooo, I wrote yet a third note and placed it into the botheration basket, complaining that I really did want to spend more time with him, and somehow magically I did get called for another appointment.

I joined the second group the next day. I simply remember sitting there in stillness, not knowing what we should say or do. He seemed to act as if he too had nothing to say. So he just started asking us our names. When he got to me, he paused, sat in silence for a moment and then smiled and repeated my last name. That's all I remember. And then we were let out, perhaps given some sweets on the way.

After awhile, I truly began to enjoy the course. Not only the guru, but there was a very handsome head teacher, the meditations were powerful, and the music was ecstatic. It took us to higher states of consciousness and I in fact loved the soulfulness of the music. It felt like East Indian meets Black American Spiritual music to me (years later to find out that South Indian Tribal music is very much that!).

Although the course was in silence, there were still nonverbal connections being made throughout the week. I noticed a few black men in the course, whom I had never seen in our local Satsang, and there was one white guy who I had a strange attraction to. I must admit, most of these men were not only observing silence, but there was also a powerful quiet energy of respect present in each. Never really checking me out, or so I thought. I was amazed that especially for this one white guy, I never actually saw his eyes. His head was bowed in meditation and respectfulness for the guru's presence, every time I saw him. Yet, for some reason he stood out to me amidst the 300 participants. I was aware that his seat was in the back middle section of the room, while mine was on the far left, mid-front. I always seemed to prefer that section in Satsang.

By the time the course was nearing its ending we were all pretty blissed-out. I remember the last day before we came out of silence. For some reason, I found myself with one of the black guys, I think he wasn't observing silence as he was an "old timer" and I think he had an ache and I must have told him that I was an energy healer, but somehow I offered to do some energy work on him. We sat outside in the sun after a lunch break. I stood above him, and he sat on a bench

21

in front of me. I shared a healing treatment with him, which I did semi-professionally at UCLA Medical Center. I remember standing in the sun, working on him, non-touch; and out of the corner of my eyes, I noticed that white guy walk by, stop and lean up against the wall about ten feet from us. He just kind of laid back and absorbed the moment.

Soon, it was time to go back into Satsang. We ended the session, went in and took our places. I remember that we were all sitting pretty close together, with just a little room behind and on the sides of each of us. The guru came in, and we began the meditation. I don't remember much more, except that what must have been towards the end of the session, I felt an energy within inches of my back, directly behind my head. I froze and came out of meditation simultaneously, and without taking a breath, heard these words whispering into the back of my head – "I LOVE YOU, I LOVE YOU, I LOVE YOU, I LOVE YOU." The words I have always wanted to hear - my whole life. And as I turned slightly I either saw or knew that it was that guy who I thought had never ever looked at me. The man I had been attracted to. Exactly what I always wanted, a man who I wanted, telling me he loved me. But, before I could fully comprehend what had occurred, the guru must have gotten up indicating Satsang was over. I tried to rise to my feet but I was still so shaken by what was occurring that I could barely move. By the time I could stand up, the man had already gotten up, and followed the guru out of the hall. Gone.

I melted into nothingness. Pure awe, bliss *and* disbelief. Entranced, I finally rose up to go out and see him, to connect with him to make real this unreal event. But before I could get out of the hall, people were coming up to me talking as silence had ended. Men, who I guess had been waiting to meet me the whole course, were now all around me wanting to know who I was and grab my attention. But I could barely talk, still reeling from what had just occurred, but at the same time happy to meet and speak to these new friends who I had obviously observed as well, during the week.

After awhile people began to leave, I didn't see the man anymore, and I had to return home, but I made a vow, that on the morrow, the last day of the course, I would make myself known to him. Absolutely. I went home and could barely sleep playing over and over again in my mind, the magic of that moment. Had it really happened? Had I imagined it all? I still couldn't believe it.

The next morning I awoke ready to face him head on. I had seen his name on his badge. No more of this being attracted to someone in my mind. After all, he had actually spoken the words. I went to class, excited for the final day. When I walked in I immediately noticed that the group was much smaller and didn't understand why, and I didn't see the man. When the session began, the first thing that was announced was the bus schedule to the airport. It was then 10:00am and as they read off the list for the 8:30am bus, his name was called out. I was stunned. I could not believe it. I sat there trying to listen to the rest of what was being said, but felt hopeless, how could he be gone? How could I be left so unfulfilled after such an incredible moment? How could something so profound be left incomplete??? I didn't have much time to think about it or wallow in my disbelief, as the class was beginning.

Instead of surrounding the stage, we were called to meet in a big circle in the back of the room. Soon I found out why, the guru had already left, as did many of his closest followers, all of those "in the know". That was why the group was so much smaller. So now led by that handsome head teacher, we gathered in a circle to share our individual reactions and feelings about the course. One by one, about 100 of us still present, went around and shared our experiences. At first, it was a little difficult for me to get into the flow, given my disappointment, but after awhile I settled down and gave my attention to each person sharing. By the time it got to me, I was sooo happy to say how wonderful I thought it had been. In an extremely jovial mood, I said I loved everything! I loved the guru, he was 100 percent loving, 100 percent beautiful, 100 percent spiritual, 100 percent sexual (I remembered hearing almost a gasp in the audience as I said this, but I was too filled with enthusiasm to consider my words) and 100 percent fun. They were the truth. He was a very sexy many. And then I added that I loved that gorgeous head teacher and the music and that basically it was ALL GOOD - to me!

We continued around in the circle with people sharing their hearts and minds and experiences. I remember this really handsome man, I had noticed him in the course. Sooo tall and beautiful and filled with that special energy that comes with that kind of package. But, I noticed when he began to speak that he was quiet and somewhat somber. And then his words began, about his child who had been in a traumatic accident and had been recovering for the past few years. How he had taken him all over to doctors and hospitals and how his heart ached as they passed through that journey. And then he said, but finally there was one day, when he was about to give up, his despair so deep at his son's lack of progress, his fear and pain was taking over. He told how he passed a bus stop on that day, and on it were the words, which he whispered so deeply and mysteriously, in the exact same tone and inflection that I had heard the day before "I LOVE YOU, I LOVE YOU, I LOVE YOU, I LOVE YOU." He said that he recognized the guru calling to him, and after that, the depth of the pain in his heart was lifted forever. My heart stopped. The enormity of his words came running thru me. Through my mind, through my heart, through my consciousness, oh my God, it was HIM. Oh my Lord. *He* had picked up that man from out of his seat, walked his body across the room, and close, oh so close *he* had him whisper to me what I have always longed for......... Instantly my body jumped up from its seat, ran outside and kept running and running until I was nowhere to be found, and I fell down and sobbed and sobbed and sobbed. In just those few moments, this Being, revealed to me that he was EVERYTHING, everything that I had always prayed to, everything that I had been intimate with for years. In that moment he brought me closer to Jesus Christ, because I then knew, how the omnipresent, the omniscient and the omnipotent could BE inside of a human man. The body is human, but the consciousness is the Divine ALL.

Chapter Two
Prelude to India

Over the next year, in addition to completing my doctorate and graduating, I was very busy attending local advanced courses, and beginning to organize courses in the black community. I realized how much stress and anger had been released from my life and felt that I must (even though I lived a little far away in Malibu) share these teachings with black people, as I was one of the very few Black Americans in the organization. I felt good about doing it because the course was separate from the guru. I could teach this stress reduction course without trying to influence anyone's spiritual choices. That, I felt was between them and God or guru if that be the case.

During this time, I was well aware of the impact that he had on most of the female teachers. They were all in love with him. But I didn't feel that way, I was simply trying to be the best teacher of his course that I could be.

He was coming back to Los Angeles and I set up a talk for him in the heart of the black community, a landmark building owned by a famous black TV star. A few days before, I also held a meeting at the Malibu house for him and African-American spiritual leaders who were unable to come to the event. As I toured him around the estate he was quite impressed and whispered to me that this could be his "hideaway." I had heard that he loved to swim and invited him, but there was not enough time. The afternoon meeting was a success and I moderated the informal group, much to the surprise of the advanced teachers who were present, who later commented on how well I had done. As I had been an administrator for over 14 years, I was surprised at their surprise. The evening event, although small, was also successful and I had the opportunity to introduce him on stage that night. When it was over, as I sat on the stage singing with a group, someone whispered into my ear that the guru was on his way up to my house for a swim. I jumped up from my seat and rushed to my house to be there.

About 15 of us, including his sister, were there that night. She and I had a good time, laughing and talking. He and only two other of his top teachers swam; the rest of us stood by in awe. Later we had dinner (he had dinner in a private area of the balcony and then joined us). Standing on the beautiful deck, overlooking the unblemished hillsides and the moon shinning on the waves below, he turned, looked at me and started walking directly towards me; but as soon as he came near, I spoke first, and said to him, "Even the moon is out for you tonight", and his body without a moment's hesitation made a U-turn and walked completely away from me. At the time, I did not understand, nor was I bothered, but in hindsight, I know that he was coming towards me and my masculine energy stepped in and pushed him away.

There was also a large advanced course organized for him in Santa Monica during the days, and in the evenings he was giving a series of public lectures. As at the Malibu course, small more intimate groups were organized to meet with him. We met outside in a circle next to the building as the larger group meditated inside. It was a typically beautiful sunny L.A. day.

My daughter was with me that day, perhaps they were having a teen course or activities planned, but for some reason she joined me in our group circle. About eight of us sat in the circle listening to him and watching him question each person. Until that moment I had never considered asking him anything; it was not in my mental make-up to ask someone else for advice, but for some reason that day I did.

When my turn came, I told him that I was aware that there was going to be an advanced international course in India the following month and wanted to know if I should come. He looked at me, paused as if thinking for a moment, kind of slapped his leg and said, "YES, definitely come!" Of course, I was aware that I had left my job and had very little money, but that was quite irrelevant in the moment.

Our time ended and our group went back inside. I think he saw one or two more groups and then it began to get darker outside and it was time for the next session to begin. For some reason he began with questions and answers, which I had never seen him do; but it was a relaxed late afternoon, the group was only a couple of hundred and so he appeared to be a little less formal or structured. It felt more like we were sitting in a very large living room with him.

I sat with my mind wandering off about going to India and how I might get there, and yet at the same time peripherally listening to him and the questions being asked. In the distance, I heard someone ask a question having something to do with energy or energy healing. And from that same somewhat distanced space, I heard him slowly begin to answer and then pause and then I heard him in a more focused voice say "Isn't that so?" I looked up and saw that he was looking directly at ME. I was dumbfounded, I literally could not believe my ears, I couldn't believe what had just occurred. HE – was deferring to – ME??!!

Immediately, I became conscious of the fact that I *was* an energy healer, but what did that have to do with anything? – HE, was the Guru, He was the all knowing. He NEVER asked anyone else for their opinion or acted as if they/someone could know more than him.

Time stopped. I was transported to another realm. I went completely out of my body, gone from the room. *Everything* went black. At the same instant, the back of my head was opened into an expansive space of infinity filled with the stars and the entire universe. I was absolutely absorbed into the blackness and the light of the cosmos. I have no idea how long I was held there. But at some point from the farthest reaches of this vastness, a bright light shone out into my mind, a beam of light so powerful, potent and yet utterly filled with peace. It gleamed out from the space behind my head through my skull and out thru the opening of my eyes, straight through to HIM sitting on the stage. There was a magnetic pull from that endless point in the universe, through my eyes to him. Three points making a divine and perfect line. Never, had I had or considered the possibility of such an experience. My eyes became magnets, lasers, radiant beams with one, and only one target; the guru. From that point on, and over the next few days, my eyes carried this powerful potent energy. I followed him as he walked off the stage. I went outside and beamed my rays on him as he walked to his car. We were energetically attached as if touching him with my entire being as he stepped into the vehicle.

I made it to my car, drove to the house where he was staying, and a smaller group of us were able to be with him after the Satsang. I sat down on the floor with the others and waited for him to take his seat, still deeply within the current of this magnetic experience. I sat bathed in that inner glow and powerful love that had filled me from this powerful radiance. Once he was seated, I paused and then slowly lifted my head and allowed my eyes to shine upon him. He was immediately absorbed in my gaze. His eyes were pierced by this power revealing itself through me. I watched him from behind this force trying to do his best to gaze at all of the others who were also present, but the moment his head turned in my direction he couldn't turn away from my gaze. The connection was so powerful, that one of his very close head teachers jerked his head around revealing an extremely jealous look to see *who* the guru was looking at in such an alluring and intense way, as *his* gaze was as potent as my own. The teacher turned and saw it was me. The guru, aware of his noticing, moved his gaze on to others. This dissipated the exchange somewhat. However, I was very unaware that this was only the beginning of a multitude of problems this man/teacher would cause for us both.

The next day, when visiting another Southern California teacher's home where the guru was visiting before taking off to Northern Cal, my eyes remained lit by the universe. A woman who I was speaking to before the guru came down from his room, said to me – "Your Eyes!!!!!" I replied. "I Know…." Those magnetic eyes stayed with me throughout the following day, when he was giving a talk at a college in Northern California. I remember loving him with them after the talk as he was giving Darshan (Blessings) to attendees. As I shined on him, I felt that that was my reason for being. As I had been an energy healer for so many years I thought that there was nothing else for me to do in life, that my job was to energetically hold a space of protection around him. *That* was my reason for being as I shined on him from afar in the crowd. But when I found myself starring at him and I saw his big eyes look up at me immediately after the thought, he starred at me and I perhaps misinterpreted his stare, one of billions of times of ambiguous interpretations. I thought he was looking at me like, "No, don't do that, don't stare at me, don't be obvious", but I was farther from the truth than I could have ever known. I believe, he was acknowledging my thoughts and saying, "YES, that is your job. That is why you are here. Finally you get it." And yet I had it all wrong. My years of Catholic and familial guilt, I had been told by many that I always interpreted things as if I was at fault. And as a result, from that moment on, *I left my place of where I was supposed to be.* I withdrew into my own insecurities about men. My lack of knowledge of what they wanted and what they meant and what their signals were about. My lack of female knowingness on how to be with men caused me many many problems in this lifetime. It made me not be the woman I was meant to be. But, that is one of the reasons we come on earth, to fill in the gaps.

Chapter Three
My First Trip to India

*I went to India because I was completely and absolutely
in love with the guru. I was in love with God. I went
because there was a course – Shivaratri; the day or week
of celebrating Lord Shiva. The God of Gods in Hinduism.
Shiva the magnificent. Shiva the transcendent. I went
because my heart was in India. I went because there
was nothing else for me to do but go to India: the calling
was absolute. I went because I had been there before
many many times. There was no place else for me to be.
However, the first time I went this lifetime, I was not aware
of that. I had been in the ashram a few days and an older
woman came up to me walking down the lane and said
"You're Indian! You're Indian!" She stared at me with
those looming dark eyes, even though she was much much
shorter than I, the power in her words hung in the air
between us. She put her finger up to me and insisted that
I was Indian. I had no idea what she was talking about.
And of course she knew I was not, in this lifetime Indian,
yet she insisted. A few weeks later, I was walking down
the streets of Bangalore and another older woman came
up to me and said "You've had a lot of past lifetimes as*

an Indian!" Once again, I did not understand what they were talking about, even though I knew about past lives, I did not comprehend it, their words did not strike a chord, but they saw something that I did not know at the time.

I arrived in India on a first class ticket, courtesy of my uncle who worked for United Airlines. He met me at the airport and saw to it that I was seated in first class. Riding in coach was the woman from L.A., whose home the guru always stayed at. It had been arranged for me to be with her as she was being greeted and received as a special guest of the guru at the airport. So, even though she was being given the royal treatment by the guru, I had flown there first class *and* received that same treatment.

He had a young man pick us up from the airport with his driver. I was pleasantly surprised to see such a young man in a position to have a car and a chauffeur. He took us to his apartment in New Delhi where we stayed overnight awaiting our flight to Bangalore. I was surprised that it was only an apartment, because in America, only the wealthiest of people with extremely large homes, have chauffeurs. India was already different. However, this handsome young man entertained us well and we were very much cared for by both his cook and driver. I was quite impressed.

A day later we boarded our flight and went on to Bangalore. I don't remember having any idea of what I thought India would be like. I had never ever considered going, so there was an absolute innocent mind as I stepped off the plane. I don't remember if it was the smells or the sights, but I know it was different from anything I could have possibly imagined. Poverty was extreme. Even the worst areas in the states looked nothing like it. Beggars were everywhere; stores were built out of tin and homes out of straw or sometimes cardboard. But after seeing his apartment, I quickly realized that there was a vast difference between the externals and the internals. Also, I had learned long ago, never to judge places by how they appear on the outside. I simply was aware of the differences between India and America.

We had our taxi stop in town on the way in order to pick up a few simple cotton Indian Punjabi Suits, to wear at the ashram as had been recommended that we wear white, simple clothes. I remember feeling concerned as we left our luggage in the taxi as we went into the shops, something one would never do in the U.S., but he assured us it would be okay. We then headed straight to the ashram. I remember the woman who I was traveling with said that she could "feel" *him* as we got closer.

The ashram was beautiful although my accommodations were quite sparse. I was housed in a cement dormitory room with about eight to ten other women. As I had no expectations, I didn't know that it could be any different, so I did not complain.

The course was wonderful, and we were well cared for. And as the home that I rented and oversaw in Malibu was in escrow (for the second time so I did not cancel the trip because again there was no guarantee that it would sell), I was only able to attend the first two weeks of the month-long course. But I was happy to attend the ashram portion of the course (the actual Shivarathri celebration) and forego the last two weeks in a place called Rishikesh (which I knew nothing of at the time).

On my first day, as I was walking around the ashram I ran into his Sister. She was so happy to see me, since she hadn't seen me since she had been at my home in Malibu the month before. We laughed and talked and I remember her saying, "Oh Kamala, you are soo funny!" She asked how my accommodations were, I said "OK." She then asked where I was staying. When I told her which room, she looked concerned, I guess, as she knew how beautiful my home was from her visit. But immediately one of the ashram ladies whispered something in her ear, and she kind of said "okay" (I suppose she told her that I was there on scholarship.)

She asked me had I seen the guru yet, I told her no. I explained to her hat people said it was hard to get to and into His house. She retorted, "Well, he'll want to see YOU!" I said, that I didn't even know where his house was, she then told me exactly where to go, and I went. She was right, I did find it easy to get in to see him. His house was small, white, quite simple yet beautiful and filled with statues and flowers. There were many people visiting with him, but when he saw me, he smiled and was quite welcoming. I simply enjoyed the moment of seeing him again.

The Shivarathri course was an experience; an international course for which he wanted us to have a grand experience of India. He made everything wonderful, including a beautiful tour of South

India. We went to Mysore the town with a Palace, which the guru said was equivalent to Versailles in Paris.

On the way, we stopped at a beautiful hotel and were individually greeted at the entrance by their staff, who performed an arti (a blessing ceremony, in which we were encircled by a candle) and then placed a garland of beautiful flowers around each of our necks. We felt like royalty. The palace was magnificent filled with spectacular rooms of gold, jewels and art. Even doors and chairs were made from precious materials. Our guide who had come with us from the ashram was a very tall distinguished man who shared the history of the palace and showed paintings of the guru's great-great grandfather who had lived there. I remember one day a few days after the tour at the ashram, that same older man who had been our guide walked up to me took my name tag, which was hanging around my neck, into his hand, stared at it, and then walked away. Later, I found out that he was Pitaji, the guru's father. I just remember feeling how blessed we had been to have the guru's father as our guide and I didn't even know it at the time; I would have paid more attention to him. Curiously, I never even questioned why he had handled and viewed my nametag. I had also seen a very beautiful tall slim older Indian woman walking with the guru and had assumed that she was his mother. One day, a very tiny older woman came up to me unexpectedly and like Pitaji, took my name-tag in her hand, looked at it carefully and walked away. A few days before the course ended, I found out that the tall woman was not his mother, but in fact, this small woman who had held my name-tag, was in fact she.

The course continued with wonderful Satsangs, sumptuous vegetarian meals made especially for us, and appointments could be had for Ayurveydic treatments, right there at the ashram clinic. My favorite of which was a "Shirodara" in which warm oil was slowly dripped on the forehead for almost an hour. It was deeply relaxing and healing, I was in awe of all that India and the guru had to offer. He had thought of it all.

Chapter Four
My First Saree

During the second week, I went into town to shop with some of the other ladies. I very much wanted to purchase a saree to wear for the Shivarathri celebration. We went to a very expensive shop, with teak and glass walls surrounding every inch of the interior. I had never seen a store anything like it, well of course that was true of all of India, and this look was especially intriguing. The closest thing that it felt like to me in America was an old library with wood from floor to ceiling, but this was modern and teak, not oak, mixed with glass, quite exceptional. They served us tea and coffee as they pulled out the most exquisite fabrics, ream upon ream of silks and beads and sequins. Colors that I had never imagined existed. India, I found out, is a garden of fabrics. I later concluded that since they had been wearing one style for thousands and thousands of years – a saree, (unlike Americans who change our styles every six months), they had become masters of color and designs of fabrics beyond our wildest imagination.

Earlier that week we had taken a drive for some reason out into a very poor village on the outskirts of Bangalore, perhaps on the way to the Palace in Mysore. I remember seeing how impoverished the area was, as the houses were minimal thatch huts or made out of old pieces of metal, but I distinctly remember seeing the women walking down the road, carrying their pots on their heads or in their arms and thinking "Oh my god, they all look like goddesses" in those exquisitely colored sarees draping their slim figures.

And so, here we were in this shop with a beautiful and brightly colored menagerie of fabrics. I remember thinking that I had been a pretty subtle dresser. My years in New York City and Bloomingdales and Saks Fifth Avenue, had made me somewhat conservative, but always stylish. However, as I held up these brilliant colors to my frame, I could in no way settle for something subdued. It was an impossibility. I decided on the most fabulous burnt orange silk saree with beading all the way down, both on the palou (the end of the saree that hangs over the shoulder) and on the skirt of the saree. The color was magnificent next to my skin; there was no way I could not buy it

The evening of Shivarathri, two lovely Indian women wrapped me in my saree. They knew just how to fold and tuck and adjust and then pin it tight; snug and secure. I felt so comfortable, so ----beautiful, and even though there was a slight shyness present about being in this unusual dress, I was immediately at home in my exquisite gown.

As I walked towards the Shivarathri gathering, through the huge crowds, there were many glances, stares and even "aahhhs", until finally two men in their early 20's approached me saying, "Excuse me Mam, you look sooo beautiful in a saree" as they resumed their bowed head stance.

I remember later an Indian woman coming up to me on the streets whispering in my ear "No Indian woman has anything on you in a saree." (Which I understood to be an extraordinary compliment especially because of the pride with which Indian women hold themselves and the garment.) I know that I have never looked better in any outfit, than I do in a saree.

Standing at the entrance of this immense gathering, I was so impressed by just how many people had come to see him. People from all walks of life, larger than any gathering I had attended in the states, instead of hundreds, there were probably two to three thousand in attendance. It was one of the biggest nights of the year, I was told he would dance, dance the Dance of Shiva – Nataraj (Lord Shiva in his dancing mode). The guru might actually allow the god to come thru him, take over his body and dance. It was an all night celebration, and everyone was beginning to settle in.

When I arrived, he was already there, seated on the stage. I guess I had taken too long to get ready. Everyone was seated on the ground. I looked for a friendly face to sit next to, and slowly made my way through the crowds and found my spot. However, as I was about to sit down, I looked up at him on the stage and saw something I will never forget. When he saw me walk in wrapped in my saree, his eyes literally rolled up into the back of his head, his head fell backwards in his seat and all that you could see were the whites of his eyes. I was astounded. Overtaken with emotion in response to his expression of emotion to me, I thought and felt that it was one of the most wonderful things my eyes had ever witnessed. Blush is not the word for the impact that his guttural instinctual reaction had on me.

Slowly, he began to stir. He had a basket of flowers next to his seat, he took one in his hand, held it for some time and then looked out at the crowd and eventually threw it to one of his American female devotees, one who had been with him for some time. She automatically reached up with her arms to grab it. Slowly again, he took another, paused and pondered over it, and again looked out into the crowd and threw it directly to another one of his old teachers. Finally, he took one, contemplated it with his eyes and raised them, looking up directly at me, but somehow, even though I had just seen that extraordinary show of affection with his rolled eyes, I still could not comprehend that he would actually consider throwing one to me. And so, my arms did not reach up to receive him, and looking defeated, he turned and threw it to another woman sitting not far from me. I felt utterly and completely inept as a woman.

Chapter Five
The Devi's Visit

A few days later we were told that The Devi was coming to the ashram. We were given instructions on how to greet her. It was necessary to shower and dress in clean clothes before going to see her. We were to line up at a certain time depending on our last name or number, which had been given. When we got in the room we were to bow down, sit and be quiet while waiting for our turn. And finally, to have a question ready that she would answer. I was very much looking forward to meeting this special woman. There was so much excitement in the air.

I with so many others from our international group waited in line for my time. I imagined an exquisitely beautiful woman dressed in a beautiful saree with lots of gold necklaces, bracelets and earrings. As it was finally my turn, I entered the building, not far from the guru's home and was taken aback, when instead of a beautiful woman, I saw two men who looked like villagers who had been working in the fields, in the front of the room, holding a three-foot statue. I couldn't quite believe my eyes, as I took my seat on the floor and continued in the cue watching each person one by one go up to the group, bow down to the statue, ask their question and the men would turn her upside down and use the pointed crown on the top of her head to write in a pile of sand, answering each question, which they then interpreted.

I watched in amazement, aware of the men appearing dirty

and sweaty and grunting as they lifted the statue, time and time again. When it was finally my turn, all I can remember is scooting up in front, asking a relationship question about the younger man I was loosely connected with at the house in Malibu, and receiving the answer, I know not what. When I was finished however, I immediately felt a strong energy overtake me. I could barely walk away, and so I went towards the back of the room and almost fell down and sat next to a few others, in a trance-like state. Having been an energy healer for so many years, I was aware of altered states of consciousness and yet was surprised at just how powerful this energy was. I stayed seated up against the wall for maybe ten to fifteen minutes until I felt as if I could at least stand up. Still under this powerful influence, I raised my body, walked out the door and headed immediately up the stairs towards the guru's home. I *knew* I had to be there with him.

I was allowed up the stairs leading to his home without effort. And when I got to the top at his door, it opened and I was permitted to enter. He had only a small group in his house. I sat with those present and eventually he called me up to him. He said, "Kamala, you went to see the Devi??" in a somewhat playful and inquisitive voice. Still in a bit of a stupor, I replied "yes." He then asked, "What did you ask her?" I told him about my question about the young man at the Malibu compound. Immediately and with the fiercest voice I had ever heard come out of his mouth, he began a torrent of words like "YOU COULD HAVE BEEN PRESIDENT OF THREE COLLEGES!!! YOU COULD HAVE BEEN......!! YOU COULD HAVE BEEN....., IF IT WEREN'T FOR YOUR OBSESSION WITH MEN!!!!!" I was shocked out of my trance state by his inundation. I didn't even know that he spoke like that - almost violent, definitely angry. However, I was in fact also stunned by the accuracy of his words, men or rather the lack there of, had been the focus of my internal emotional life and yet I had had no idea, prior to his words, just how much those concerns or, as he said, obsessions had cost me. As soon as he indicated that he was through with me, I got up and left his house.

I began to withdraw into my own insecurities about men, my lack of understanding of what they wanted and what they meant and what their signals were. And so by the end of that first trip, I began to become very angry with him, because prior to coming, we had had that unbelievable experience of the light of the universe shining through my eyes to him, on him, in him through him. And I guess I had expected more of that kind of connection with him, but it seemed like I was receiving nothing in the days that followed.

And so there came a point where I had watched him walk in one too many times with his entourage of women that I had had it. I was mad, I was angry, and I wanted to go home. I sat there in an afternoon Satsang and all I could think about was going back to Los Angeles. "Humph!" How dare he not give me his attention? What was the point of me coming if not to actually be with him?" And as I was lost in this mental tantrum, I heard him speak out my name from up on the stage with 1000 people present, "Kamala, thinking about L.A.???" I sat stunned right out of my daydream. The woman sitting next to me, a head teacher who I knew, turned to me to see just what I was doing. And when she saw the look of guilt and embarrassment on my face, she was horrified. She looked at me as if thinking, "how dare you!", that I could have been sitting there thinking about Los Angeles, instead of having all of my attention on him. Of course, I wasn't thinking so much about L.A., as it was about me wanting to "get out of his presence!" And so, he played his games with me, knowing that I was very upset because I had only been able to come for two weeks of the course. But now my two weeks were up and that was what made me finally feel my anguish. I didn't express my frustration early; like always, I waited until I couldn't take it anymore and until it was time for me to go. And so, I blushed with embarrassment as he read my thoughts about wanting to leave him.

Finally, it was in fact my very last day. I waited in line to go into his home to see him. I was allowed in, and I sat in the back of the room of about twenty-five people, as one by one he called each of us up to talk to him personally. I was very upset, as I hadn't spent any time with him. We hadn't connected. And as the crowd dwindled down, he finally called me to him. I got up and went to his seat. He said in a soft and sweet but almost sarcastic voice, "So, Kamala, coming to Rishikesh?" Immediately I broke down and screamed sobs at him that," NO! No! I am NOT!" I told him that I was not going to Rishikesh, that I had only come to Bangalore, that it was time for me to go back to California and that I hadn't seen him, that I hadn't spent any time with him and that I was so upset. He immediately laid my head in his lap and let me cry and cry and cry and eventually he said

"It's getting better isn't it?" And I continued to cry, but softer, and replied, "nooooo."

And that was how I left, that was how my first trip to Bangalore ended. I went back to my room, packed my bags, caught a taxi to the airport, and boarded a plane to Delhi on route to the U.S.

On that plane, I sat next to a young Indian woman in her early 20s, and we had a nice conversation. She asked where I was coming from and I told her that I had been at that ashram. She immediately turned to me and said that she had heard of him. She heard that he had a big house. I told her no, it was quite small. *(Later, I sadly came to realize that I had never actually been inside of his house, only the outer receiving room.)* But then she looked me directly in the eye and asked a question that no American could even fathom to ask: "Is he God?" I stopped, went inside myself and replied, "YES". *She knew, what we did not, that some humans, not just one, could in fact merge with the Divine*

When I arrived at the airport in Delhi, I shopped and spent all of the remaining rupees that I had left, as I was about to catch my connecting flight to Los Angeles and would not need them. When the flight was finally called, as I had flown standby via my uncle's gift ticket, I of course had to wait until all the other passengers had boarded the plane. Remaining at the gate were about a dozen of us waiting for our names to be called. I noticed an older Indian couple that looked quite tired and distressed. Within a few minutes of the regular boarding, I realized that they had shut the doors to the ramp. I looked around, and finally went up to the counter and asked what was going on and was told that the plane was full and that no stand-by passengers would make it. I was stunned. Never in my entire life had I missed a flight.

Hearing the older couple talking, I went to ask them what had happened. He said he worked for United and had been turned down on a flight for two days. There was another airline that had gone on strike and so all seats were full. He was told *they* couldn't expect to get out on stand-by for another *week*. I tried to comprehend what he was saying, realizing that I was only a *relative* of an employee and if an employee could not get on, then my chances didn't look very good.

I went down to the lower level to call the States and let them know that I would be late. I needed to let my daughter know and speak to the owner of her dance studio who she was staying with for the two-week trip. My other friends had also wanted her to be with them, but, when I telephoned my daughter and then spoke with the studio owner, she insisted that Krystal stay on with her family as long as necessary, so all was well. I also needed to know if in fact the house in Malibu, which I managed, had actually sold. It had been in escrow before and did not sell, and I needed to know how urgent it was for me to get home. I called one of my housemates to find out that YES, it had sold and we had to have all of our things out of the house in one week. I began to panic. I HAD to get back. I HAD to get on a flight.

Immediately, I began going to ticket counter after ticket counter to see if I could get a flight to another city, pick up a United flight there and then fly to the States. Each agent tried to see if there was a flight on which I could connect, but no one could find a seat. Eventually the counters began to close as it was getting closer and closer to midnight. Or, the employees were simply nowhere to be found. They kept suggesting I try another airline, and so I waited and waited and waited. Finally they began to propose that my best bet was to go to the ticket agencies in the city the next day. That it would be easier to get a flight there instead of at the airport. That made no sense to me, but as each counter repeated the same thing by 3am, I was exhausted, stir-crazy and starving, as I hadn't eaten since breakfast at the ashram, I began to acquiesce. Earlier, the older couple had suggested that I sleep at the hostel at the airport and take a taxi into town the next day. I would have gone to a hotel; however, I had spent almost all of my rupees at the airport shops buying gifts before I got on the plane, and I had very little dollars in the bank, with which to replenish.

Fearful and defeated, I dragged my way to the hostel at three in the morning. There were men sleeping outside on the way and I was scared, but I made it there and went in. I was soooo hungry, and they had a counter serving food that was still open. It looked very dirty, but I was starving. So I ordered a bowl of dahl. After all my time in South India, I thought the food was hot there; NEVER in my entire life had ANYTHING been as spicy hot as that bowl of dahl. I cried as I forced it into my mouth, thinking only that since it was soo spicy that it would burn away any possible germs I might get from eating in that filthy place.

I dragged all of my luggage up to the sleeping room and there were maybe seventy to a hundred cots with people asleep on them. I found one empty bed near a couple and with my shawl covering the sheets and pillowcase, I laid down and collapsed in terror.

Thankfully, I did sleep, awoke the next morning hearing the couple next to me discussing taking a taxi into town to go to the travel agencies. I got up, brushed my teeth, washed my face and asked them if I could share a taxi with them, as I was almost completely out of money. They agreed.

I was dropped off in front of a building where I was told the United Airlines office as well as a number of airlines were housed. I climbed the steps in the dirty downtown building, which was maybe four stories tall. As I entered the United offices I was happy I had come early as there was no line, an unusual occurrence in India. I went directly to the counter, spoke with the man on duty and he, like the men the night before, attempted to search for a flight. He told me about the strike and that there were no seats. Disappointedly, I asked him what I could do, he said to perhaps try another airline and look for a connecting flight thru a different city, but he doubted it. I traveled up and down the steps of both that building and a building a few blocks away, one by one being told the same thing, that they could not find a connecting flight. After a few hours, I returned to the United office, exhausted, and tried one more time, to which the man in a very unIndian-like manner shouted at me "LADY, THERE ARE NOT SEATS – GOODBYE!" Exhausted, stunned and spinning, I stumbled backwards, and laid up against the wall. My mind was slowly trying to trace the steps of what his words meant: "There…are…no…seats, I…can't….get…on…a…plane, I….can't….get…to… America, I… can't…. get… to….the…house, I….can't….take…care….of…my…. things….at…the….house. etc….etc…. Slowly, it began to sink in; the impossibility of it, and yet the reality of it. And equally slowly, I realized I had no idea what to do.

I walked down the dark stairwell, out of the building onto the streets stunned by the brightness of the daylight. I dragged my body which again had not been fed, down the busy sidewalks, in a fog, when finally I remembered that I had the card of the young man who had originally picked us up from the airport and housed us some two weeks before. I searched around in my purse, located it, walked still dazed until I could see an STD box (what a phone booth is referred to in India);I picked up the phone, using the few remaining coins I had left, and was relieved when I heard his voice on the other end of the line.

When I shared with him as best I could what had happened, he immediately without hesitation told me to get in a taxi and come straight to his house. He gave me the address and told me that he had to run to an appointment, but that his sister would be there to meet me. In a stern voice he reiterated – "Come straight here now!"

Overcome with relief, I followed his words verbatim. I saw a taxi, hailed it, told them where to take me and immediately collapsed into the back seat. The ride was not long, and as we drove down the somewhat familiar small lane that I had seen not too long before, I looked up and saw the most beautiful woman standing on the balcony, smiling and waving down at me, and for the first time in my life, I prayed that she, this unknown woman, would have all the answers to my problems (I had never given up my power or even desired to give it up in this way), as I could not even begin to think or fathom how any of it could be handled. She came down, gave me a hug, paid the taxi driver and slowly led me up the stairs.

She had tea waiting for me, her face, the room, the table was the very opposite of the turmoil I felt inside: absolute peace and calm. After I had caught my breath, she asked that I share what had happened. As I poured my woes onto this unknown woman, she sat there extending her presence of calm, as if knowing that was in fact what I needed the most. After I had finished, she sat, gazed out the window in front of which we were having our tea, considering it all and eventually turned back and with a wise voice said, "Oh, I see. You were meant to go to Rishikesh." I was preoccupied with my daughter, California, the house, my finances, didn't have the ability to extend my knowing beyond all of that to anything that she was saying. But as I listened to her, she revealed that she in fact was in charge of coordinating all of the bus arrangements for the group coming from Bangalore in two days, continuing on their course to Rishikesh. And that she understood that I had been *sent* directly to her.

I was somewhat taken aback by her words, but still more confused by all of the responsibilities that I currently was overwhelmed by. She said, simply to use their phone, call America, make sure my daughter was okay, I told her she was; asked me was there someone that I could borrow money from, I said yes; and finally we discussed the issue of my furniture needing to be out of the house and somehow I remembered that the owner owed me back monies, and that I could have him use some of that money to hire helpers to put my furnishings in storage as I had already packed up most of my things, just in case.

Immediately I picked up the phone, telephoned my college friend and she said she would happily put $200 into my bank account; called the owner, told him my situation and he told me he would take care of it; again, phoned the friend who was watching my daughter and told her it would probably be two weeks before I could get a seat, and she said it was no problem. In a matter of minutes, *all* had been resolved. This goddess said that she would book me a seat on the bus; we would meet the group and the guru in two days at the airport and get his approval on my continuing with them. I was amazed, as she had in fact answered my prayer uttered less than an hour ago in the taxi – All was done!

The next two days were wonderful. She toured me around New Delhi; there had not been time on the way in. I got to see India in all of its splendor. The parliament was beautiful and equally impressive with massive buildings and grounds, the architecture looking very much like Great Britain, heavily affected by the years of British rule. Such a grand imprint they had left; the expansive lawns, great buildings, so unlike America. She also took me to see ancient forts, throughout the city, reminding of the heavy and ancient Muslim impact on the country and of their military power and might.

She took me to meet and have dinner with her friends. We went to the beautiful home of a journalist and his wife, I can remember sitting there listening to his laugh and the jokes he and his friend were telling and thinking, *Where am I? He sounds and looks so much like my uncles in America, very black looking and feeling - soulful, very much like family.* The women at the dinner were wonderful, beautiful socialites, and yet so Indian with each of them bringing dishes from their regions of India, wanting to impress me, as well as convince me that their state or area had the better tasting dishes. I was so at home.

Soon, too soon as we had many more things we could have done together, it was the day the group and the guru were arriving at the Delhi airport from the ashram. My new friend had already reserved my seat, but we needed *his* okay for me to attend the course on scholarship and of course to re-join the group. We went to the airport to await their arrival, all 300 of them. As they walked into the terminal from the plane, those who knew me were quite surprised to see me. A few asked, "but I thought you were gone back home..??" One by one, I gave a brief synopsis of my adventures, waiting for the guru to come out. First I found the head organizer of the course, explained to her what had happened and that I wanted to continue to Rishikesh on scholarship. She said, that she would have to ask the guru, so we went in different directions in search of him. Eventually I looked over and covered almost to his nose in garlands, I saw him, light beaming from his eyes, completely immersed in Spirit. I tried to wave, and at the same time I saw this same female teacher whispering to him, and from across the room, without looking at me, actually seeing him look through me, he acknowledged. "Yes, she can come!" And again – it was Done!

I got my ticket, kissed, hugged, cried and thanked my new friend for ALL that she had done for me, and headed toward the row of busses waiting to carry the entire group to the next part of the adventure: Rishikesh. As I got into a line, I immediately saw a handsome man who I had met the night of Shivarathri. I remember choosing to sit down on the grass with a group of women surrounding this attractive man. They were deep in conversation; however, the moment I sat down, he turned away from them, began a conversation with me, and we never parted. It was as if we had picked up our conversation from a former lifetime without skipping a beat. On the periphery of my consciousness was an awareness of the other women as this was such an unusual occurrence for me. Usually I was the one in which men turned away from, never the one who grabbed their attention. But that distant awareness was not enough to make me stop, WE were so obviously connected and in our own world. And so of course, here he was again waiting in the line of the bus. He asked if I would sit with him on the bus ride, and we re-joined our centuries old conversation, whatever it was, as if we hadn't been interrupted, even for the past few days since Shivarathri.

As we sat chatting away enjoying the very very bumpy ride, a moment came when my words were stopped in their tracks, as I felt a powerful vibration come over my entire being. I paused mid-sentence for some time. Finally, I turned to him in all seriousness and said, "I don't know *where* we're going, but it *is someplace very special.*" Again, having been an energy healer for so long, I was quite conscious of the physical effect that this place in which we were headed or had entered, had on my being. Even though I had never heard of it before, I already knew that this place called Rishikesh was extraordinary.

Chapter Six
Rishikesh

We arrived at our destination and were told that the busses could only go so far. We had to walk, carrying our bags, across a bridge that was actually *on* the river Ganges. *On*, meaning, straddling the river on barrels just a foot or so from the water. We walked shakily as the river rocked us from side to side, sometimes getting wet, as our ashram was on the other side of the Ganga. I had never seen anything like Rishikesh. It looked like ashrams or what I assumed to be ashrams for as far as you could see on either side of the Ganges River. Walking across the water so low that it almost felt like the view Christ must have had when walking *on* the water.

There was a presence of peace, beauty, and yet, still the starkness of India, nestled at the foot of what I learned to be the Himalayas. Many people walking around in white and ochre robes, unlike the rest of what I had seen in India, which was so filled with brilliant colors. Later I found out that in the general population, white is only worn at funerals, so it was in this holy place of prayer, that people were wearing white as many of us in the ashram had been asked to wear.

When we finally arrived at the ashram that was ours for the next two weeks, it was right on the river, with a big clock tower down below in front. The grounds were interesting with lots of those brightly colored painted statues in the courtyards. I really did not care for this style of spiritual painting, too bright for my American taste, but they were all over many parts of India. It was almost like a museum in parts, with these colored statues depicting, I guessed, some sacred scriptures. When I got to the registration area, many people had already been checked in. The two women in charge, who I knew from California, said to each other "What will we do with Kamala?" (as I was such a late add-on and had no prior room assignment.) I heard one of them retort, "put her with the Indians." Almost as if throwing all of us brown people together into God knows where, was the feel...... *It was not the last time I was to hear that phrase.*

Contrary to anything they may have imagined, I ended up being roommates with a tall beautiful, brilliant Indian woman from Dubai. We had a marvelous connection both on the intellectual and emotional levels. She was a journalist, who wrote about political topics affecting the country. She was also a wife and mother and we shared our stories of being tall women in a world where female height can often be damaging to a young girl's and woman's self-esteem.

The course was more than anyone could have imagined. Pure bhakti (love love love) although at that time, I had no idea what that word meant. I remember when we were in Bangalore, he started a Satsang one day by saying, "So what would you like to do?" And people responded with different ideas: let's go here, let's do this or that. But here, after two weeks with him in the south and then a few days in this magical place, he simply walked in one day in a total dream-like state, seamlessly sat down and alluringly said *"Sooo, what would you like to do?"* .....Not a sound was heard and he was well aware, that sitting there looking at him and being in his presence, we were All, *doing* what we wanted to *do*...... The power of his love had come inside of us, in full force.

Our time in Rishikesh was also quite the adventure. I think there is no place like it. So stark and yet so powerful. So deeply spiritual as it is nothing but ashrams and little spiritual shops, for miles up and down the Ganges. Filled with ancient prayers and traditions; one of which the guru told us is to take a bath in the Ganges at 4:00am, dunking our heads three times under the water. On a number of early mornings I did just that, by myself in the moonlight.

One beautiful day, he decided to take a large group of us for a dip in the river. In modest India, we were told that the women had to go in with their full sylvar kameez (dress and pant suit) on, while of course the men could go in in their shorts. We all happily complied, carrying a change of clothes and a towel. He led us to the river, the men in one area, the women in another and we met in the water facing each other. We laughed and giggled at just the idea of being in the water with him. It was pure bliss. Then he said on the count of three we were to submerge ourselves in the waters. And like little kids, a state in which he often had us feeling, we all went under, once, twice and then I guess I must have come up quickly on the third time to see him, standing there, simply viewing us (he had not gone under this last time) and was taking in our joy..... I was deeply moved by his warmth and delight of simply watching us.

Another day, he took a group to the Ganga, we were told that women on their cycle could not go in, so as it was mine, I did not, but I went to watch and be present. I sat on a rock with about ten others, above the river, not far, and watched him swim up and down with maybe forty or so devotees mimicking and surrounding him. When he was finished, he stepped out of the water. I, and a few others immediately pulled out our cameras to take pictures of this brilliant wet glistening god, in trunks and tee shirt. However, he immediately shouted "No", and his eyes widened like I had never seen before and we promptly set them down. When I returned home and developed my film from the trip, there were many frames that were completely whitened out from those snapshots that I made in that moment, with only two in the series, which were actually viewable. I remembered how his eyes had opened when he looked at us and was once again, amazed at the extent of the powers of this god-man.

A few days later, during a mid-day Satsang, he took us through a very deep meditation. In it he had us expand our energy field, from a few feet in front of us, in back of us, above us, and below us. Then out to the edge of the room, then the neighborhood, the planet, and finally the cosmos. In that powerful meditation, I became one with the entire universe. Pure bliss... beyond belief. It was an expansiveness that I will never forget. I truly was one with everything. As I sat there in absolute peace and splendor, I could hear him at the edge of my mind, ending the meditation, which would simultaneously end Satsang. But as I was one with the All, I had no desire to come out. And so I decided to just stay and bathe in the cosmic bliss. After awhile, however, I became aware of a very potent pause. At which, I opened my eyes to find him turned completely away from the audience facing me on the side of the stage, staring me straight in the eyes. And I realized, he wanted me to come out of meditation. So, I came out, and the moment I did, he stood up and began to walk down from the stage out towards the exit. I was standing on the side of his route towards the door, when he arrived at the place where I was positioned, he halted his exit, turned directly to face me standing less than a foot away, looked straight into my eyes, raised his finger and powerfully pointed to my heart, only a few inches away from the actual organ, and then turned his finger around and even more forcefully pointed back at his own, and with a "hmph!" sound, closed his fist over his own heart. Then he turned and walked out of the building. I stood stunned, first from having come back from such a high place in consciousness in the meditation, but then to have the intensity of his energy tear through my entire being. I tried, with the little bit of strength that was available in my legs to turn and follow him out of the door, but by the time I stepped outside, I could no longer stand. I sank to the ground and sat on a step, unable to even consider all that had just occurred, what he had done, what it meant, or who I was. A half an hour later, I regained my strength and attempted to go up to his house. But instead of an opening, which one would expect from having had such an encounter with him, I was again turned away at the door by his people. Frustrated and confused, I backed off.

The course continued with beautiful Satsangs and powerful energies began to exchange between he and I. One evening, while meditating, I felt a powerful and intimate energy slowly and intensely welling up in my body. I allowed it to take me over sensually and entirely, and when I came back to earth, there he was on stage; his eyes were glazed but he was looking in my direction and speaking in a voice of a lover who had just come out of his own ecstasy. After that, there were continual encounters, in which he chose my body for his pleasure, but always from afar.

It was the last day of the course. I remember hearing that the guru was taking a group on a jaunt up the Ganges. I tried to find where they were, but to no avail. But it was wonderful exploring the upper regions of Rishikesh, which I had not yet seen; more jungle-like than down below, untamed and uninhabited, but very beautiful with small cozy beaches. A few days before I had visited the old ashram of Maharishi, the guru's former guru and realized that was where both he and the Beatles had dwelled. Eventually, I decided to turn back and go and get ready for the final evening's festivities. I would wear my saree again, and knew I needed extra time to prepare. I went back to my room and my wonderful roommate helped wrap me and so I was uncharacteristically ready ahead of time. I decided to walk back outside and a little bit back up the path and by chance I happened to run right into the guru followed by just a few devotees. He was dressed down in afternoon walking clothes, while I was in my finery. When he saw me his eyes glanced down as if meeting a lover who was attracted *to* him, as a woman would. But I was dressed as the goddess and well aware of my own beauty and shot back at him the feminine receptive eyes as if to say, "*Oh no, I* am the one to be viewed here." It shifted his energy immediately back into the *male* mode, where it needed to be.

As I was ready early, I decided to go back and explore some of the unique shops and stalls up and down the Ganges. Walking in my beautiful saree, making sure that I didn't step in any cow dung or rub up against any of the stray cows who roamed the narrow paths, viewing the matted haired scantly clothed sadhus, I was a bit ill at ease. Eventually I made my way into one of the fine jewelry shops that was huddled between the many trinket, book and inexpensive clothing shops. I had met the owner earlier during the week and he had wanted me to come in and view his items in more detail and as it was the end of the trip, I thought I might make a purchase. He welcomed me in, invited me into his backroom, ordered tea for us and began to slowly show me a selection of his finer items as he talked on a more personal level. His jewelry was quite fine and he was quite charismatic, so much so that I lost track of time and realized that it had actually become dark and Satsang had already begun.

I made my apologies but hurried out of the store quickly making my way down the darkened lane getting to where I was supposed to be. When I arrived, he was already on stage and Satsang was well underway. Because it was the last night, everything was decorated to the finest. Beautiful flowers, ornaments, and decorations I had never before encountered. As I rushed to find a seat, far from the stage because of my lateness, I noticed something else, which I had never seen, which completely shifted my eyes away from the decorations. He was wearing a beautiful white silk robe, but with one major difference - it had a brilliant red border about eight inches thick. Red he had never been in before, at least not to my eyes. And I felt that it was an indication of the energy, which had been exchanged between us in those last few days. He looked extremely displeased to see me walk in late and as the Satsang continued on with all the bouquets and accolades given out for all those who had made the course such a success, I felt completely out of place as I had nothing to do with his celebration except be a bystander in the crowd. It was an absolute dowsing of the flames, of energy, which had been built up between us. The next morning, when I went to say good-bye, he seemed distant and simply matter-of-factly told me to get going; nothing too much more. I felt dejected and confused. I don't remember the bus ride back, the airline strike must have ended and I easily made it on a flight; but, as I was walking down the aisle, before I could get into my seat, I felt for the second time, a tremendous wave of sexual energy course through my being, somewhat like that in the Satsang, but so much more powerful that I had to fall into my seat. In fact I said to him inside, "please just let me get to my seat." He let me know that he was *very* much with me.

> *Thirty days in India. It changed my life forever. I fell in love with the absolute beauty of the Ganga. The power of the Himalayas. The mystical powers that lay there and within its peoples. But mostly I realized that India was my true home. After returning to the states I realized that in thirty days, there was not one pair of eyes that had not looked at me with love. I had never known that. Not the beggars, not the kids (who looked at me with curiosity as they knew I was not Indian and yet I was brown), not the wealthiest and surprisingly not the middle-class. Behind all the stares, there was love in the eyes, and that perspective changed me. What it felt like at the end of the trip, was that my body got back on the plane, but that my heart had been taken out of my chest and planted in the earth of that beautiful continent.*

During the next few months, I continued my work at UCLA Medical Center as an energy healer. But, it had changed. I had changed. I noticed immediately that not only were my hands simply perfect magnets to whatever the injury or illness was, but upon my immediate return, I saw that it was no longer necessary for me to even use them. I simply stood behind my patients lying on the table and gently waved my head from side to side as energy poured forth from my third eye. Something profound had opened up from within. It was also during this time that a message began running through my mind. It was like a mantra chanting its way into my consciousness, "You are my wife, we come here every lifetime and every lifetime I have to remind you who you are." Over and over and over again, until eventually I began to both believe and succumb to its power.

Chapter Seven
The Car

Coming back from my first trip to India I stayed with friends for a short time while my daughter was lovingly offered her teacher's home until I could get settled. One day I ran into a friend who was and is a "Real Man". I think we had been in India together or we simply had connected deeply at an advanced course of the breathwork. But he had that masculine air of "taking charge" taking responsibility and making things right. When in passing I happened to mention to him that the Malibu house had sold and that I came back from India to no home, he couldn't believe it. He immediately said, "You can stay with me." I knew that he had a girlfriend, but he said they had an extra bedroom and bath and insisted that I stay with them. Also, his girlfriend often house sat at an estate in Malibu so they were away a lot.

So, to my new home I went. He came in his truck and picked up my things as I had no vehicle and even put my furniture and belongings from the Malibu house, which had sold while I was in India, into storage. Everything had been let go of (or so I thought). I settled into their Hollywood apartment. I had a temporary job and was doing my energy healing work at the hospital. I took the bus to and from work and walked around used bookstores in Santa Monica, rummaging the spiritual sections. It was on one of those visits that I came across a book, which was a hymnal for an East Indian spiritual group who was now headed by a female guru. It intrigued me, perhaps because of one hymn title, so I bought it and went back to the apartment. Somewhere during this time the idea of the "kundalini" energy had come to me, possibly from previous readings, but I know the guru never used this term as he tried to stay away from esoteric language and concepts. His teachings were primarily about day-to-day living and being happy as a human on the planet; although in the past he had given talks that had been taped on more esoteric teachings in which he translated ancient Sanskrit texts for everyday use. And they were extremely powerful.

In my room that night I thumbed through the pages of this book and came across the chant "Hymns to the Goddess Kundalini" and something in me knew that I should chant it. Not knowing the melody, I simply chose a random one and tried to pronounce the words as best I could. I must have chanted for about a half an hour and soon found myself in a deep meditation. Quickly, I began to go deeper and deeper into a trance-like state and in that space, I connected to a Being, a part of me felt it was the guru and yet it also seemed like something different. I somehow realized, either from direct communication or simply a knowing, as the energies in my body were stirring in a way I had never experienced, that I was beginning an ascension process. It felt to me as though the guru was attempting to bring my vibration up to his, so that we could in fact be man and wife, as the mantra had been repeating, and in that moment I asked this energy within, "CAN THIS PROCESS BE SPED UP?" In other words, was there a way for me to get to Him/It faster? And, as the energies began to calm down, it felt to me that in that moment that *an agreement* had been made between us.

I had only been back in L.A. a week or so, when all of this occurred. The very next day, another friend from our group whose house I had stayed at the first few days upon returning to the states knew that I did not have transportation. She telephoned me to let me know that a teacher who had gone out of the country for a few months had left his car parked at their house. In the past, they had let people use his car on other trips and she did not see that it would be a problem for me to use it now. He would be gone about a month or so and had driven it in from Colorado, as he had to fly out of the Los Angeles airport. That afternoon, I went over to their home and picked it up. After doing some shopping, which thankfully was much easier than taking the bus, by evening I was headed back to Hollywood headed east on one of the main freeways in Los Angeles. I entered from the beginning of the freeway near the beach and had been driving at about 65mph for only about ten minutes, when I felt a tremendous wave of heat, a powerful energy pouring down from above through the top of my head. It was almost like molten lava coming through my skull. This energy was so heavy that quite quickly it took me over and I was out. I have no idea how far I drove before I came back to myself; perhaps three to four exits, but when I finally opened my eyelids and came around I just remember saying/thinking "I sure the heck hope *YOU* have been driving this car, cause I know I sure haven't been!" I was quite shaken, of course, by the idea that I had been on the freeway unconscious and eyes closed for *any* period of time, and I quickly pulled off the freeway and proceeded to take the streets home.

Slowly, I made my way across town and to the apartment building. I found a parking space directly in front of the building, which was rare as that part of Hollywood was like an apartment jungle and there were never enough parking spaces for all those who lived in the buildings, often requiring a walk around a block or two to find a space.

I went into the building, still quite shaken and feeling a bit befuddled, but I was definitely grateful and feeling safe to be "home". The next morning I awoke ready to attend a one-day course with the group. I prepared myself with backjack (a support for your back when sitting on the floor), blanket, pillows and water ready for a day of breath and meditation. As I walked out the front steps of the apartment building, arms full with all of my supplies, I looked up and was startled by seeing an empty space at the place where I had parked. I stood stunned and yet almost immediately went into a state of shock. Fear began to take over as my eyes looked up and down the street that was jam packed with cars as far as I could see, with only the one empty spot on the entire block right in front of my eyes. I tried to make sense of this seemingly senseless situation, thinking, "well I was quite groggy last night as it was an *unusual* (to say the least) evening, perhaps I'm confused and actually parked it down the street." I began to quickly walk down the street in one direction and then back in the other, searching for a car that I could not find.

Eventually I went back into the building, sat down and decided to call the police. The officer who I spoke to said that I would have to come in and file a theft report, but said he would take the license plate number over the phone to begin the process. I told him that I had just borrowed the car and that I had no idea what the number was. He told me there was no need to come to the station until I had the number. He also suggested that I call the impound company as perhaps it was parked illegally and got towed. That felt good to me, as I thought it might be difficult to get the license plate number. There was only one tow company for the area and I telephoned them, and of course they asked for the license number, when I didn't have it they were willing to take a description, but quickly told me that nothing like that car had been turned in overnight. Completely embarrassed, I realized that I had to call my friend from whom I had borrowed the car, hoping that she had the license number. When I phoned her, she was shocked and immediately said that they did not have the number. I asked her for the teacher's contact number in New Zealand and that I would have to call him and get the license number direct. She gave it to me but I, of course, was aware of an alarm in her voice. I asked her to *please* not tell people about this as I was aware, from the experiences of the night before, both the energy on the freeway and the meditation with the guru, that he was involved in some way. I thought that there was something working itself out, and that the fewer people who knew about this the better. She said she would do her best. I hung up and directly called New Zealand, unaware of the time difference. When a man answered extremely groggy and told me that it was 3am, I felt really bad, but still asked for the teacher. He replied that there was no one there by that name, I confirmed that I was calling the correct number and that it was in fact New Zealand and he said yes, but he did not know of that person. I apologized and hung up. "Now what to do???" was all I could think.

After much praying, it occurred to me that the Colorado Department of Motor Vehicles should have the license plate number. I got their number, telephoned and explained the situation and asked if there was any way that they could get it for me. They told me they could only give that information out to the police. I then called the police station back and they said that it was Saturday and they were too busy and that they probably could not get through to DMV and that I would have to wait until Monday, I pleaded with the man, but he just said, "No." I hung up the phone and the weight of the circumstances began to hit me that this man's car was lost, and I was responsible, and I just began to cry. Not a cry of terror, as I was still knowing that the guru was in charge of this circumstance, but just an aching from not knowing what to do.

Later that afternoon after resting for awhile trying to bring back some sense of equilibrium, I decided to call the police station yet again. This time I got a black woman officer. I explained my plight and begged her help in retrieving the license plate number. She paused and with a voice of compassion, responded, "Let me see what I can do, I'll call you back." Thankful beyond words, I hung up and waited. Within an hour, she telephoned with the license plate number, which she had gotten from the Colorado DMV and told me to come down to the station and file the report. I happily jumped on a bus, went down to the station and did just that. All of this happened on a Saturday, and I simply had to wait and be patient and try my best to go about my business as usual, as there was nothing more for me to do. Monday morning, the telephone rang and I was surprised to hear a hefty voice on the phone. "Is Ms. Easton there?"

"Yes", I replied, "this is she".

"This is Sheriff Johnson from the Colorado Police Department, you filed a missing automobile report?"

"Well yes I did, sir."

"And could you tell me what was inside the car when you last saw it?"

Somewhat confused, I replied, "Officer I don't remember much being in the car, I think it was pretty empty."

"Well, we have found the car, here outside of Denver, and it was full of stolen property. We captured the thieves and have them in custody!" his voice filled with bravado. He reminded me of movies of the sheriffs from the old Wild Wild West who had just captured an outlaw.

Stunned and confused, I asked him again where he was calling from and he informed me that the town he was in was only about 20 miles from where the owner of the car, the teacher, lived. That the thieves had stolen the car in Hollywood and robbed homes along the way and ended up outside of Denver where they had been apprehended. I explained to him that the owner would not be back for three weeks and he told me that that was no problem. They would hold the car there for him with no impound fees and he could simply pick it up when he returned. Astounded, I asked him if there was any damage to the vehicle.

He replied "Nope, it looks like it is in mint condition", still boasting with every breath.

I thanked him, hung up the phone, sat down and tried to recapture all that had occurred in my mind. This teacher's car had been picked up from outside the apartment, driven almost 1000 miles, back to his neighborhood and was safely awaiting his return. It was more than my mind could comprehend. I immediately telephoned my friend who had loaned me the car, told her the good news and that I would purchase the teacher's one-way ticket back to Colorado when he arrived. And it was over. As I tried to take it all in, it became obvious to me, that the Divine did not want me to be driving as the intensity of my process had begun

Chapter Eight
In The Middle

Over the next year, I began to notice that whenever I was in Satsang with him present, I would go into a very deep deep meditation. The first time this happened was in Lake Tahoe at my first Gurupurnima Course (Gurupurnima is the day in which most Hindu's world-wide celebrate their guru). I don't remember much except that as his eyes closed, and went into meditation (which he normally did at the beginning of Satsang and would stay in that state for fifteen to twenty minutes), mine did as well as I fell into a deep state of consciousness. I have no memory of what occurred during that time, except that as my eyelids lifted from their heavy place, I noticed that he too was coming out of meditation. The next day, however, when I was in the bathroom getting dressed, an Indian woman directly spoke to me and said, "I know you didn't see, because your eyes were closed, but I SAW HOW HE LOOKED AT YOU! Umph!" Because I was so innocent, I had no idea of what she was speaking, but apparently his sister did see as well, as from that day on, she, the woman who had befriended me so at my Malibu home and at the ashram in India, refused to speak to me and forthwith began to cause me much pain, embarrassment and anguish.

Towards the end of that course, I noticed that the sexual energy began to intensify again, usually when we were in small meetings with him. In one gathering, I noticed a tall beautiful blonde, exhibiting seemingly erotic responsive energies to the same waves of heat that I was feeling. I very much wanted to know if she was feeling the energy that he was sending towards me, or if he was directing it to her as well. I did not know. I did not ask, but I didn't like it. Once again, I did not have an opportunity to spend time with him. They kept his home hidden, but on the last day after most had left, and we were outside having a small meditation with him, he jumped up at the end of another heated exchange and said that he would cook the rest of us dinner, and invited us all to his house. That evening as I walked to his doorway, for the first time knowing where he was housed, I entered and immediately there he was, standing in the kitchen stirring a pot of food - those big eyes staring straight at me only two feet away. I was taken aback by the shift of seeing him normally up on the stage and far away, to him being only a foot away and in such a mundane and realistic situation. As if a young girl, I almost fainted as I passed by him taking the scene and those eyes into me. I had to go and lay down. One of the other things that I loved about the guru was his earthiness. Perhaps it was simply being a South Indian, but there was something very instinctual about even his physicality and his ability to verbalize with very few words. As we returned from this Lake Tahoe trip, the caravan of cars stopped at the home of a devotee in the bay area. It was so exciting to be in those cars, and I was driving. Almost getting lost, I got to the woman's house after the larger group. But when I entered the room, he was already seated on the sofa with a group about to watch television. He moved over to make a space for me to sit. And then, picked up the remote, as everyone was waiting for him to choose the channel, and handed it to me, with simply a "hmmh" sound. So guttural, but saying so much.......; allowing me to have the control.

During this phase, I hardly remember my life in between courses. Being with my daughter, trying to make a living, doing temporary work, staying from place to place as it was difficult to settle down without a job. But overall, really only listening to my inner voice, which said to be with him. I can remember one Satsang in Los Angeles, when it was announced that he was soon to come to town, my entire body broke down in inconsolable tears, as it had been completely exhausted from not being with him. I didn't even know that I was that wanting or that much in love. But my body revealed itself.

Over the next few months, I began attending more advanced courses in the Los Angeles area, continuing my assistant teaching of his course and beginning to take the teacher training courses so that I could be a full teacher of the breath course; and at the same time, falling more and more deeply in love with him. However, I also began to feel an overwhelming sadness and longing for him, both when away from him as well as when I was at a course with him, but not *with* him. It became so intense that I began to cry almost on a daily basis as my heart ached for him so deeply. I shared this with no one, as I felt utterly alone in these internal goings on as well as never having been accustomed to sharing the depths of my pain with anyone.

One day, I read in the local paper that an author who had written a book about modern day love, yet based on the love between Radha and Krishna, was coming to a bookstore in Santa Monica. He was from Oregon and was a Hari Krishna; but as I was falling so deeply in love with this Hindu saintly man, I thought it might be helpful in my understanding of what I was going through. There was a small gathering, perhaps twenty or so of us, but his message was beautiful. He talked about Lord Krishna and his consort Radha and the power of their love and he briefly spoke about "Krishna Consciousness". During the middle of the lecture, when there was some chanting, I became overtaken with a beautiful and powerful energy. So intense, that I felt the need to get up and leave the group. I went down the stairs and found my car and sat. And, for the next hour, I was enraptured; filled with a love of pure bliss. It was one of the most powerful and beautiful experiences I had had, and what astounded me, was that it was without the guru. It made me know, that I could love "God."

"God Only" in these beautiful and ecstatic ways, with or without him. And I felt empowered.

I let him know this new found power, and either by e-mail or in person, said to him, if he did not want me as a woman, it was okay, because what I really wanted was GOD. He gave no reply. But I remember saying this to one of his closest teachers, crying to her that I just wanted God! She looked at me with surprise, and asked me, "Did you say that to the guru?" And I replied yes, but still to no avail.

It was around this time, that I began to notice, when on one advanced course, while deep in meditation, my right shoulder began to twitch. At first, just a little movement, but soon it began to shift from a twitch to almost a reflexive yet continuous jump. So strong, it stirred me out of my deep meditation and I opened my eyes to see if anyone could see what was going on with my arm. Slowly and steadily, I looked around and saw that everyone else had their eyes closed and were completely unaware of me, and so I allowed it to continue as I could tell that I had control over whether or not stop it. This was the beginning of regular happenings of energetic twitches, my arms being raised up in the air, and my head and neck moving from side to side, while meditating, but never to the point of anyone noticing, so I simply allowed it to happen.

Chapter Nine
I Must Be Crazy!

A month or two after Lake Tahoe I decided to attend an advanced course at the Montreal ashram. It is magically set in a pristine forest an hour or so outside of Montréal in the small town called Trois Rivers. I arrived a day early and so the ashram was quiet; only the staff that lived there was present - about four or five people. It was very nice to get to know them on an individual basis in such an intimate environment and to truly feel the vastness of the property. The woods were mystical and the cabins that we stayed in were rustic and fitting for the environment. I settled into my cabin knowing that eight to ten more women would join me soon, but at least I got to select my own bed and asked what I could do to help prepare for the course. The lovely young married teacher who ran the ashram told me to just enjoy myself and that she was thinking of an assignment for me. Later when I returned, she smiled at me and told me she was giving me a job that everyone wanted. I had no idea to what she was referring. And then she said, "You can clean the guru's house...it is a job that everyone would like, but I'm going to give it to you!." I was elated. Never in my wildest dreams, especially as somewhat of a newcomer, did I think that I would be in his house and get to clean it.

She led me through the woods, down the path to his small white two-story home. It was simple, pure, and clean. Immediately I felt very much at home in it. Matter-of-factly she began to show me around the house, almost as if it were just any house. We toured the living room and kitchen downstairs bedroom and bathroom. She told me that these were the rooms that I would primarily be in charge of cleaning and that someone else would clean his rooms upstairs, but she was kind yet again and took me upstairs and showed me his bedroom. Cautiously, we walked up the small spiral staircase, and entered the room. It was small and had a very interesting bed that was raised in the air. She explained that he had it built up high so that when he woke up in the mornings he could see out of the high window and have a view of the forest and the moon and sky at night. And that actually, it had been built more than once, until it came out just as he wanted it. We returned downstairs as she gave me my final instruction concerning cleaning the windows and to have everything spotless, but she did not go into detail as to how I should clean; she said she would leave all of that up to me. I so appreciated her kindness and willing openness in giving this gift. It was heaven. Again in her generosity, she told me that I could take the next two days to clean it; not to rush so that I might surely enjoy it and be thorough in the process. And so, there I was in his home alone caring for it, and although I was still quite naïve, there was no way that I could not appreciate the specialness of this gift; the intimacy of this gift. And so I began wiping every cupboard, dusted every knick-knack, swept and mopped every floor until it felt complete. While I was there, two men - one was the husband of the woman and the co-manager of the ashram - came in to clean his room. They looked somewhat surprised and a little annoyed to see that I was there, but they did not bother me.

A day or so later, he arrived. Word spread that he was having an afternoon Satsang. And so I hurried to dress to get there. When I arrived, the room was already full, about 300, and he was seated on stage. I willingly stepped over a few people to a spot about six rows back and on the far left side of the room; as the front was packed. However, as soon as I did, that voice which had begun speaking to me in my mind said, "Come up front." I was stunned. There was no way that I could feel comfortable climbing through that crowd to squeeze-in, in the front, with those all of those people. Again, but more insistent, "take a seat in the front!" I replied in my mind, "The only way I could do that is if you would make a space up there, then I would come." Within a moment, of this psychic interchange, a beautiful Indian woman who was sitting directly in front of him - first row, center - got up and left. What was I to do, but get up and finagle my way through the crowd, all the way to the other side of the room, all the way up front to that seat. And as I did, he smiled.

The course became fun, with lots of exchanges of energies and lots of flirtations. I felt like a young schoolgirl, giddy with that new sense of love and excitement. I remember after one encounter, I ran back to my room to change into something special for him, and encountered my former roommate from Malibu, as she asked me something about the guru and his availability and I cockily said, "The guru is mine!" A very confident and unusual attitude for me with a man, but he had done enough to make me know he wanted me.

That night at Satsang, was a very unusual evening. For some reason, roses were for sale before Satsang, so that we could offer them to him for the special celebration. I was guided by that internal voice, for which by now I was sure was his, to purchase one. No longer afraid, I went all the way up to the front of the room, and sat down in the front row just a few spaces to the right of his chair next to a man that I really liked, and his beautiful wife and sweet two-year -old daughter. Soon the guru entered and sat down as usual. And as usual, when he closed his eyes, my eyelids became heavy and they too closed. About five minutes into this meditation, I heard the voice in my head say, "Touch my foot with the rose." Shocked out of meditation by this statement, I immediately opened my eyes to see something I had never seen before, instead of his legs being completely covered by his white robes, as they *always* were, there dangling in front of me out from behind their white curtain, was his right foot which must have been crossed over his left knee. He however, still had his eyes closed and appeared to be deep in Samadhi. I was stunned. Even though I had let him push me around to that seat up front that first day and a few other things that week, I said inside, "There is *no way* that I am going to get up from my seat, walk up to you, and touch your foot with this rose!" He must have laughed inside (knowing the eventual outcome), because again he said in my mind "Touch my foot with the rose!" I was stymied, filled with fear and apprehension. But my ego *knew* I had to give in. He was making me muster up the courage to do things that *I* would *never* do. "Miss Play It Safe"!

And then, it was as if everything in the room stopped, time

seemed to stand still, like I was moving through a sea of energy which I had never felt, all in slow motion. One moment at a time, my head began to turn and there before me stood the little two-year-old. And I guess my mind or his mind registered its fear to do it alone, and instantaneously saw a way that I could. With the same still motion, my hands reached over, gently took her into my arms and slowly offered us both with the rose in tow to the guru's foot and tapped it gently with the rose. Within a second his big eyes popped open and he immediately pulled up his finger as if to indicate "No, don't do that", but the same second that it was about to point down towards me, he caught and stopped the movement of his finger when he saw that it was me. Everyone in the room was frozen with disbelief, including me, as well as the parents of the child. Inside, my being was saying "Huh, what just happened?????" But then, the energy snapped back into present time and he continued Satsang as if nothing had happened. Later that night, I saw the dad and apologized for having used his child, but he said, "It was all surreal, and I just let it happen as it happened. I was aware that something otherworldly was playing out." I was so relieved that he understood, although no one I think truly understood; and that he was not upset but in absolute oneness with the moments. The next day while in my cabin, a teacher who I had overheard a few days before talking to the manager of the ashram about a strong seemingly exciting energy that she had been experiencing, approached me. She said that she had just come from a teacher's meeting with the guru and that the guru didn't want to say anything to me, but that I should be told "Not to ever do anything like that again!" referring to touching his foot while in meditation. I was livid. Hurt that he would talk about me in a teacher's meeting and livid that he would say things about me given that he had been prompting my every move. When she left the room, I sat down took out a notepad and decided to write out my anger in a note to him, finally revealing everything that had been going on with me.

I completely let my words come out as if he did not know what I was talking about. I told him about all of the sexual energy exchanges, and all of the psychic communications. I told him that if it was not him doing these things to me, then he needed to refer me to a doctor, because "I must be crazy!" I sent the note off to him, and the very next day was told to come and meet with him. A first. Going up late in the afternoon, outside of his house was absolute stillness. No people were loitering around trying to get in to see him. I think people thought he took afternoon naps and so did not disturb him. I knocked on the door at the appointed time, and it opened much to my surprise by one of his closest teachers, a heavy set woman who was a great yoga instructor. This woman, looked at me, smiled, said hello, and lifted her hand in the air for me to magically enter as she walked out the door with no additional conversation. As if magically, I wafted into the room, which felt completely still and somewhat dark, at just that beginning of evening in the late afternoon, after the day, but not yet the night. Standing directly before my eyes, was the guru, who I assume had just had a yoga class, clad only in cream colored, cotton knit body fitting leggings and a matching body fitting t-shirt. His long black hair hanging loose down his back; he was drop dead gorgeous, I was completely taken aback, and yet at the same time, smiling from head to toe.

He motioned for me to take a seat, and as I did, I saw that there was an Indian woman dressed in a saree sitting on the floor in front of his altar on the other side of the room. Immediately she broke the beautiful stillness of the moment by going into a tirade, in Hindi. I can only surmise what she was saying because he immediately *yelled* back at her with a "hmmph", in English, "She can be here!" The woman then got up angrily and left the house. The next thing I know, he walked up the stairs, saying that he had to get ready for Satsang. I sat, taking in what had occurred. It seemed clear to me, that if he didn't want me, he would not have let a woman who had said the things that I said in the letter, come in and see him as I did, nor would he have screamed at the lady. But before I could think too much, I heard the phone ring and he answered and began to talk, but while he was talking, the sexual vibrations which I had come to know and love so well, overtook my body in an aggressive manner, much stronger than ever.

When the energy subsided and I regained my equilibrium, I could hear in the background that he had hung up the phone. And soon thereafter he came downstairs dressed in his white robes and immediately said, "Come, we're late for Satsang" and led me out the door to be immediately greeted by throngs of people who had been waiting to escort him to the hall. Stunned, not only by the crowd, but by all that had just occurred, I ran to catch up to him and the crowd and forced my way to him and demanded that he answer the question in my note and tell me what I should do. He paused, and then responded , "Get a job." I paused, and then shouted at him "Get a Job???!!!" and immediately broke down in uncontrollable tears. I thought, *"What kind of an answer is that???.* I just stopped, found a bench, and continued to scream and cry. He paused for a moment, and perhaps sent someone back to console me, but then he just went ahead with the crowd to Satsang. Eventually, after crying for almost a half an hour, I got up and drug myself to the Satsang building, and there sitting in the kitchen was his teacher of teachers, a very wonderful woman who I had a wonderful connection with. Breaking down again, I shared with her the intimacies which had occurred energetically between us in detail, and her response was "Oh no, not *you*," as if someone she thought was special had also succumbed as others had to his mystical powers. She questioned whether I was confusing the feelings and that perhaps it was simply my second/sexual chakra opening, but, as I described in detail, her voice lowered as she admitted, "Yes, I have heard this before."

Chapter Ten
Soul Birth

The course was over and many had left the ashram to return to their cities. About forty or so of us were accompanying him to an afternoon talk that he was giving at a Canadian Hindu Temple not too far from the ashram. Our group was primarily made up of teachers and a few people from Montreal and the local area. We were told to be on our best behavior as it was the first time he was attending this temple and wanted us to make a good impression on the members of the community.

As we entered, everyone in the temple rose, realizing that he too would be coming soon, and merging together we all formed two long lines on either side of the entryway creating an aisle as we awaited his arrival. I was three quarters of the way down on the inside line closest to the hall and as we were a large group, I stood back a bit allowing the temple members to stand in front as to have a direct view of him as he entered.

I can remember seeing his body step through the doorway, but after that momentary view, all was a blur. It must have begun as he neared me, as almost immediately, I, my body; yes my body, began to *cry*. Perhaps it began in my head or eyes as crying usually does; however, it soon began to spread throughout my entire being. I felt as if every cell in my body was crying. I had absolutely no control as I was completely overtaken with this and well there were no words- sensation? I had no idea what was happening. I had never experienced anything like this in my entire life. After a few moments I felt the crowd move into the gathering room and my body moved with them. I could see that our group of teachers moved to the left side of the room while the congregation sat on the right. My body went with our group and somehow I made it to the floor and sat. However I was still crying uncontrollably. I saw out of the corner of my eye that the handsome head teacher was sitting near me and I caught a glimpse of him looking very annoyed with my inability to contain myself. I noticed him look up at the guru as if to say "What to do with her?" and somehow I noticed the guru either wave his hand or simply imply to leave me be. Still unable to stop this absolute uncontrollable weeping, I took my shawl, covered my head and lowered it to the floor, hoping to muffle the sounds and be as inconspicuous as possible.

Around me I could hear the singing; and at some point I guess the singing stopped and the guru started speaking, but I heard none of it. I was totally captivated by these experiences going on inside of me. There was nothing for me to do, but ride the wave and BE. Eventually, maybe an hour or so later, the Satsang must have come to an end, as I heard rustling and realized that everyone was standing up. I just stayed with my head down and let them leave the room, as I still was unable to compose myself. After awhile, my body eventually calmed down, and I was able to get up from the floor. When I realized that the room was completely empty, instead of leaving and joining the group downstairs, I walked towards a back room and took a seat in a chair. I rested for perhaps five minutes when, *my body*, with no volition from me, *stood up*, (I was quite aware that I had not stood it up), and then *on its own*, *walked* across the room to the window on the far wall. When I/it stopped, all I could do was KNOW that for 45 years, *I* had *walked* this body, and KNEW that I was well aware of what it was to *choose to walk*. But I had *never* experienced my body *being walked* on its own.

> *From that moment until this day, my life has never been the same. It took a few years or so to understand that that moment was the actual realization of my godhood. That that vibration was the entering of my godself into my being. My merging with the All The extent of that*

expands with time I bring it in with fullness and as I allow
the imperfect, injured human in me to release. And, I Am
That I Am..

No sooner did I have these thoughts, did my head lift itself up
and look out the window and point my eyesight directly on the guru
below, standing outside of his car. I was aware that this was unusual;
it actually looked as if he was waiting for someone. So taken over by
what had just occurred, not so much the hour or two of uncontrollable
crying but by my amazement of my body moving, that I could not
consider much of what was going on outside. I placed myself into a
highly alert state, watching and perceiving everything in my sensory
realm. After about five to ten minutes of standing at the window eyes
fixated on him, I saw him finally let someone enter the empty seat
in the back of the car and he stepped into the passenger seat and the
car drove off. Still unable to feel or grasp what was occurring, just
in a state of amazement and yet absolute peace and calm, I simply
observed.

After a short time I heard people coming back up the stairs and
into the room, which had earlier been filled. Again, I watched as this
body of mine, moved itself out of the back room and into the main
hall, where I saw twenty or so individuals who had returned after the
guru's departure to the airport. In front of me was a small group of
three or four including a husband and wife who I had gotten to know
well. My body then moved itself towards that group. Not knowing
what I was doing, why I was joining them, I continued watching and
looking from inside out with wonder. When I stepped into the group,
the husband asked me what I was doing next and when I was returning
home to California. I told him that I didn't know and that my ticket
was not to leave for another few weeks. He and his wife then invited
me to come and stay at their house out in the country. They assured
me that I would have a good time and that it was peaceful and lovely.
Having to assume that that was why I had been brought to them, I
replied "Yes, that would be nice," in utter amazement that the next
step had been filled in without me having to do anything but allow this
energy, this force, to lead.

Eventually, we went downstairs, left the Temple, and got into
their car. First we stopped at their home in the city to pick up some
things and then later on made the drive to their place in the country.

I remember very little of this, other than trying my best to hold a conversation with them and yet at the same time, overtaken by the awareness of what was going on inside of me. That first night, when I got into bed ready to rest and try to comprehend all that had occurred, I remember just as I was drifting off, being quite shaken by the feeling of a full body presence laying directly behind me. It was so full, that at first it frightened me. It was a very strange feeling to feel the physical outline of a body as if someone were actually laying next to me, and yet not there. I remember, simply feeling and knowing that it was he in his energetic body, not understanding how he could do this, but eventually I fell asleep comforted.

A few days later, we went to a local shopping center as I needed to get a large duffle bag in order to ship all of my things home in one piece. Somehow I must have left my companions and wandered into what appeared to be an herb store (the sign on the window was in French, but it was pretty easy to make out). I entered the large somewhat dark store and saw what looked like hundreds of glass jars lining the shelves. Again, on its own, my body walked up to one of the first shelves and I watched as my arms reached up and pulled down a jar. The label was in French, and so I had no idea what it was. I continued to walk around the entire store and pulled down jar after jar until I had selected six or seven from the shelves, none of which could I read the contents of. My body then proceeded to pick them up and take them one by one to the counter. I of course had no idea how much of each I needed, so when the clerk took the jar, released the lid and indicated in French as if she was asking me how much I wanted, I just allowed her to scoop and after a few small scoops of the first container, my hand lifted up and waved horizontally in the air as if to indicate – enough! It appeared to be no problem that I was not speaking and that my hand was motioning as she was speaking French and must have just assumed that that was our best way of communicating. However it was, it worked. As she proceeded to open each jar, she scooped and my hand indicated on its own, how much was required. When finished she packed up my little bags, I paid, said "Merci", and walked out the door, amazed but aware only that my bundle must have contained what I needed.

Since that day, I have always selected all herbs, vitamins and supplements energetically by simply running my hand past the various bottles until it magnetically stops at the best ones for me. Interesting, this Spirit inside even chooses which are best for me with the consideration of my current finances, i.e., there may be a "best" product, but if I can't afford that one, It will select the "best" one for my budget as well. The Divine is perfect in that way.

The next day, the couple drove me back to the Ashram, where I had arranged to stay for another week. I was one of a small number of participants staying for an Ayurvedic course and as a result, I got my own cabin and in an area that I had always wanted to stay. I moved in, aware of the coolness in the air and happy to have my own space and on the ashram grounds to begin to take in internally all that had been going on in and through me over the past days. I began to unpack and settle in, decorating with little bits of whatever I had, trying to make it feel a little like home.

Not long after settling into my room, I felt a strong wave of energy begin to take over my body, not like that which had walked me, but much more intense as it filled my head and then my body with a heavier stronger vibration. As it began to take me over, my body began to turn in a circular motion, slowly round and round, eventually it sped up and became faster and faster and faster until I was almost spinning like a top and then with a whumph! It/I was thrown down onto the nearby bed; safely, but strongly. And as I fell with this whumph, it felt as if my mind had been shaken and loosened, as if something, an energy or perhaps even a thought pattern, had been knocked out of it. As I was quite dizzy, I laid there for some time, stunned. Never had anything so powerfully overtaken me, and yet at the same time, I was fine; just dizzy but also quite nauseous inside. These movements occurred a few more times, sometimes turning me clockwise and sometimes counter-clockwise. Somehow I came to understand that the counterclockwise spinnings were removing energies and the clockwise spinnings were placing in energies. As I was alone and no one could see, I was unconcerned about how it might appear; I perhaps assumed this was part of that "process" that the teacher had referred to. All in all, in my heart of hearts I believed all of what was occurring was simply the process of him, bringing me up to his level of consciousness so that we in fact could become man and wife. And so I just let it all occur.

Then something even more profound occurred, something that made me feel that it was separate from the guru. Slowly, I was walked to the opposite side of the cabin away from the bed and closer to the window. I felt myself deepening within not needing to care for anything. Fully being drawn into what was occurring. It felt as if the body was being pulled deep from the bottom of my feet into the ground beneath. As I stood there in this powerful/magnetized state, my eyes were drawn down to the floor in front of me. And though I did not see anything, I felt and seemed as if I saw as it was projected in front of me from the floorboards, an energy, oh so slowly worming or spiraling its way up, like a funnel spiraling its way up from the depths of the earth. Coiled and releasing like a serpent from the darkest deepest recesses of the planet. I was almost pulled to the ground as it wove its energy up and up and up directly in front of my being. And even though it was in front of me, at the same time, I felt the rhythms moving up and into my body and through me as well. And although it was dark, and deep and extremely earthy, definitely coming from below, and different from all else that I had ever felt coming from above and or into my third eye, I was unafraid. This merging of the depths of life held me in a trance for over an hour. I stood there, feet glued to the ground, and my body up and thru my eyes filled with the heaviness of what I now know to be the Kundalini Goddess Herself. But at the time, I only perceived a powerful, very dark, yet distinctly feminine, serpentine energy, like no other. I had no words for Her.

That evening there was a small Satsang for the twenty or so of us present, which included the ashram staff. With the guru no longer there, it was very intimate and quite different. But we were all happy to be there singing songs and there was a birthday celebration for the young woman who ran the ashram, who had let me clean his house. She had such a beautiful energy and I remember she selected her favorite bhajan to sing that night, one that I had never heard before, but which I immediately fell in love with - "Nataraja, Nataraja, Nantana, Sundara Nataraja". Satsang was blissful and I fell in to an extremely deep meditation. So deep that even though I was aware that it had ended, I also felt the energy hold me deep and so I stayed in my seat; it was clear that it was not time for me to go. So, I just stayed in Samadhi and let it have its way; there was always a reason. It held me for at least a half an hour or so after I had felt the room had vacated. After some time, the energy again, began to enter my body, but from my crown chakra down, rhythmically spiraling through my core. As it entered my body while seated I began to sway, back and forth and began to rotate in a circular motion as if rotating in a yoga posture. Eventually it started to slowly pull me forward as my forehead touched the floor and then as slowly come back up and bend backwards. Movements at first were not that different from our gentle yoga classes that we taught with the breath program, and as I had been co-teaching for awhile, I had been allowed to lead these simple movements with the groups. However, after awhile, my body was lifted from the floor and I began to be walked to and fro across the room. The movements, however, became much more specific. Moving in directions that I began to see were angles in relation to the guru's seat at front center. The room was large and could hold 300-400 people and my body was moved around the totality of it. Sometimes directly perpendicular, other times crisscross, but still in straight lines. Then it would stop me and place me in positions, postures that I had never seen. At one point on the floor with legs crossed, it bent my body forward and clasped my hands behind my body taking one of my hands and clasping my thumb and middle finger around the opposite wrist, holding my hands and body in this bowed position directly in the dead center of the room, and directly in front of the guru's chair. When I rose up, there was a powerful energetic connection between my being and the chair, it felt like a radiant stream, alive and active.

At another time, it took me to the left side of the room, sat me down and took me into an even deeper state, so deep that it took my energy and attention deeply inside my own body, inside my chest, down into my heart and I actually heard my heart beating from the inside out. It was beating all around me, amplified as if on a loud speaker, but I was inside almost as if I were underwater. After awhile, it lifted me from the floor and moved my body again directly in front of the guru's chair, where I could hear another heart beating in addition to my own. It was beautiful, miraculous, and unimaginable. I was held in that space for some time, and at some point the movements resumed and continued for at least two hours. Eventually, I came to a place of absolute peace, filled with gratitude and wonder and joy.

The next morning, I got up early as it was my day to teach yoga for the group. I was only allowed as the course was over and they wanted to give beginning teachers an opportunity to teach. While on the stage with about ten people taking part, the woman/

teacher whose birthday it had been, came upstairs into the room, late and somewhat in a hurry. She stopped and looked and seemingly disappointed said, "Oh, it's you", "I just had a dream where I was told that there was some fantastic yoga going on upstairs." I smiled inside at her disappointment, and realized that *that* yoga of which she had dreamt, had occurred, the night before, and wondered if the guru had sent her that message.

Although years later I destroyed all e-mails written to the guru, because when I opened them and read them, I would become energetically ill, below is one of a few that were written to others during that time. This is one to one of his longstanding male teachers.

Hi X
I am so glad to see your e-mail address on the digest. I actually tried to phone you last week, but the number that I had was not good. This has been some year for me. Following the Guru, getting TOO close, and having EVERYTHING inside, turned out. There seems to be NO ONE in AOL who can relate to my experiences. It's been the best, but it has also been at times well over the edge. And now, I just am losing my sense of trust in him. I am always overwhelmingly grateful for all that he has done to my life BUT/AND, I'm concerned that this Being who has entered me, who is me, can not be trusted.. I would love to speak with you, either e-mail or by phone. I know from your experience and from the peace in your being that you must have gone through something to get where you are. I don't know if everyone's experience is unique, or if there are some things that are similar - I have NO GURU experience. I have recently read EVERYTHING on Kundalini, and understand that I received Shaktipat in Montreal, but it has been since India that these things began. Soooooo, any words of wisdom (or any words) would be helpful.

Jai Guru Dev

Chapter Eleven
The Body

News must have spread about what I had shared with his teacher of teachers, because soon thereafter, while at two of his primary world-wide teacher's apartments, the handsome one from my first advanced course in Malibu who I had become somewhat friendly with, pulled me aside and sternly asked me "Do you have sexual problems???!!" I was completely taken aback, as I had never heard this soft-spoken man speak so harshly and also because he was blaming me, for what he had heard. I had cried my circumstances to that other teacher and she had acknowledged that it was not the first time she had heard of these things. I was shocked, because I felt that all of this had been done to me, and also hurt that he was placing absolutely NO responsibility or blame for any of this on the guru. In the years to come, I found that *everyone* in the organization did the same, never thinking it could be him. Standing up for myself, I shared with him more details of the interactions, that I had lost my car, and my home and every little thing that was causing me pain and finally with a small bit of compassion in his voice he replied, "Ah, the process has begun........" I had no idea what he meant. And no one in all the years to come ever shared what, if anything, they might have known about this "process".

However, over the next six to eight months, my life was quite the roller coaster. The movements, which had begun in Montreal were that of my body beginning to realign and transform and they took over my life. Whenever I was alone, it was in a constant state of motion. Yogic postures were held sometimes for an hour or more. Once while on a Temporary job in Los Angeles, I was in an office working and the moment the door would close and I was alone, my body would stand up and begin doing postures, a lot of which was centered around my neck; holding it back with my eyes looking upwards for long periods of time. (Years later I found out that I have an inverted curvature in my neck.)

In addition to the movements, the breathwork, which I had done so regularly began to change. My body began to breathe itself; doing strenuous and long breathing exercises, as needed. I was able to hold my breath for extreme lengths of time, without effort. I no longer needed to do the breathing taught in the course. I was breathed through.

Many of the Siddhis or gifts began to reveal themselves as well, although again at the time I did not know what they were. One evening, while sitting at my altar, I began to notice that my vision of the guru's photo began to change. At one point it became very tiny and at another it was greatly enlarged. When in groups, my hearing began to be altered, sometimes I could hear conversations across the room, and I also began to notice that people would bring me specific information that I needed to know about a number of issues, of which I would never have been privy to. My healing work at the hospital also went to another level, as I was able to bring about dramatic changes in my patients, far greater than before. Each these gifts, as they appeared through me, seemed to last about three to six weeks, and then another would reveal itself.

For a long time, I was fine with all that was occurring. Again, it was done in privacy and it never felt as if it were harming me. Until, however, I was staying at a friend's house in Los Angeles, who I knew from a spiritual group that I had been connected with years back. When I began to share with her some of my experiences, I would speak of hearing *his* voice and that *he* would do this or that, and at one point she stopped me and said, "When are you going to stop saying *he* and start saying *your higher self?*" I was taken aback by this comment, as I had always assumed that it was *he*. And the idea that it might have been *me*, was much more than I could handle. I thought, "If this is *me*, doing all of these things, then I am *mad*." Immediately I began going to bookstores and reading in depth about Kundalini. In all of my Western spiritual readings, this topic of transformation had rarely been discussed. I began to read everything I could find on the chakras, on the serpent energy, as it is called, and on higher states of consciousness. It was during this time that I opened a book on Kundalini and found a photo of a woman sitting on a floor in a yoga posture, that was the exact same posture that I had done that night in the big room in Montreal; sitting in lotus posture, arms behind her back and her forefinger and thumb grasping the opposite wrist and bending forward. I was startled and at the same time felt somewhat more secure that what I had and was going through, others had been through, and it was comforting to see it. During this time I came across another beautiful large mostly picture book on Kundalini. I thumbed through the book and was caught by surprise when I came across a full page etching in black and white of a young Buddha baby face, close up. What was most amazing was the bright red flame of fire depicted above his head. Seeing this, like many of my other realizations along the path that came from simply being with what was occurring, I understood that this was the equivalent, this drawing depicting the Kundalini energy, was the same as the photos and words that I had read many times in my life depicting Pentecostal Sunday. The tongues of fire above the Apostles' heads were in fact, their Kundalini energies rising.

Thank the Divine, that during this time of intense change, because I had not yet acquired a home and had been in Montreal and India for almost six months, my daughter chose to stay with a family near her school. As a single Mom we had never been apart before, with the exception of a few summers in which she visited her grandparents in New York. However, during the times of all of these changes, she wanted to stay in California and not go with me. I remember upon my return for some reason wanting to rent the video "Jesus of Nazareth" with Anne Bancroft and Ernest Borgnine. There were three scenes, which stood out to me in that film. One, I watched as the actors looked at the man playing Christ, and I saw a look in their eyes, one of admiration, longing and absolute love that I had only seen people in our organization look at the guru with. I wondered, *how* could those *actors* have known to look like that? The second was a scene in which one of the Apostles was packing his things about to go off and follow Christ. He says to the other Apostle, "I told my family I'm only going to be gone a short while." And the other Apostle either replies or implies, "yeah right", as to the absurdness of that idea. And the last one, may not have been a direct quote from the Bible, but it was somehow a clear message I got watching thc film, there was the scene in which Jesus says something to the equivalent of, "Come and follow me and greater things in this lifetime ye shall receive." And again, these are not scriptural words but the message that I received from it, was that I had *gone and followed him* that calling which was greater than anything I had known, and what I received was the beautiful unfoldment of my daughter, right in *this* lifetime. Before I had left, she was somewhat shy and withdrawn. When I returned, what I found was a beautifully blossomed young flower, who was much more radiant and open than I had ever seen her. I had been much criticized for having left her, but the beauty that I came home to, only confirmed the rightness of my following my inner knowingness.

I remember a year or so later, sitting in our weekly Satsang and watching a video that the guru had made on Kundalini. I was very much surprised to even see such a topic as again, he rarely spoke about esoteric terms. As I listened, he talked about the dangers of this process and emphasized the importance of the need for someone going through this should be at an ashram where they could be under care and direction. I remembered feeling so angry that no one had offered such a setting for me, and that I had been all alone and having responsibility for a child, and bills and all of worldly life, during my "process".

Chapter Twelve
Hawaii and the Mysterious Ticket

Although I had been to Hawaii in the past with my daughter, I had never visited Kauai. The guru was having a tour of Hawaii and I was so happy that I could join in. As it was the case, my funds were limited and so friends told me to wait and purchase my island hopping tickets once I got there, as I could get a better price. So off on the next adventure I went. I arrived in Kauai after a brief stop in Honolulu and went to the home of one of the devotees who rented out rooms in his home. Following a wonderful phone conversation, he ended up placing me in the best room in the house, small but beautiful overlooking an exquisite cove. When a few others arrived we immediately changed clothes to go to the home where the guru was staying and later to attend his evening talk.

We arrived at a palatial island home owned by a devotee. About thirty people were gathered at the house, mingling about enjoying the beauty of the home. The owner was a very kind and unassuming man in his early 40's. He was a long-time devotee who had moved from the states not too many years before. It was lovely being in the home knowing that the guru was somewhere about and enjoying the food and beverages that had been so beautifully prepared for all. He had begun a tour for me, but got distracted by someone and so I just continued to mill about. When, suddenly, I realized that I was at what must be *his* door. It was open and so I slowly walked in. He saw me and smiled, obviously happy to see me, he welcomed me. Slowly I walked up to him, and as we began to chat, his hand reached out and touched my hair. He said, "You changed your hair." And I replied that yes I had, it was now very curly and I think more feminine than the last time I had seen him. We exchanged a few more words and then he walked across the room into what I assumed to be his bathroom or dressing room, but he left the door open. I simply stood there, aware of the unusualness of the moment, loving the intimacy of it, when suddenly one of his close female teachers walked into the room, looked at me, then looked and saw the bathroom door open and walked over to it and closed it.

Later that afternoon while we mingled around the house waiting for him to come out, I noticed a woman, who I knew, crying in the corner. I went to her to find out what was the matter. She confessed to me that she cared for him so much and that it made her so sad to be unable to speak to him. I hugged her and tried to console her. I told her to go to him. Just go to his door and talk to him. She resisted and said she didn't know if she could. I told her to just get up and go, that people had been doing it all day and that she could too. She smiled slightly, wiped her tears and within a few moments got her nerve up and went to his door. Later, she came out with a glow. That evening however, when I saw her allowed to ride in his car and also noticed she had a look of conceit, as if she was his, I became remiss that I had helped her. Because for some time from that moment on, she spent more time with him, walked into Satsang with him and she gloated over the fact that she did. I had put myself out for her and this was my thanks; a prideful conceit never a thank you. I felt sad, that I was not with him. The only time *I* had felt as if he were mine was that moment at the Canadian ashram, right before one of his teachers told me he had been discussing me in a teacher's meeting. Never again did I have that feeling, that confidence that he belonged to me. All the times of being denied entry into his homes, rarely getting to spend time with him, squashed any sense of confidence about this man who I loved so deeply.

That night at a smaller meeting at the home, I was through; realizing that this man, god or not, still had not treated me rightly. He still had not loved me on the outside after all of this internal talk, and

I just couldn't take it anymore. I got up in the middle of his talk and ran outside and cried. I just wanted to leave. After a few minutes, his close teacher, who had found me inside of his bedroom, must have been sent outside to talk me back in. She sweet-talked and coerced me until I returned. When I came back in, I was guided to sit up front, directly in front of him. He continued his talk, smiling at me, and at the same time fiddling and playing with a little hula girl figurine in his hand resting on his lap, that he would flick with his thumb and she would flip backwards and forwards, on and on and on. I couldn't help but see the resemblance between her and myself, and others looked annoyed at the almost erotic movements of this doll.

A day or so later, we left Kauai continuing the tour to another island. We arrived at the airport, but there were two airlines, which flew between islands. I had heard that the guru was on Hawaiian Airlines and so, since I had not purchased my island hopping tickets in advance, I went away from him and the crowd to the opposite side of the airport in order to purchase my ticket. I got in a line with about 15 or so people ahead of me; I was not concerned as I knew the flights did not take off for another hour or so. When off to my right, who comes alone from around the corner, but the guru himself. I was quite excited and surprised to see him coming my way, especially without a group following him. He slowly walked right over to me and asked me, "Which airline are you traveling on?" Thinking I had a clue as to why he was asking, but somehow assuming it was not for my best, I slyly replied, "Well the same airlines that you are on, Hawaiian Air" with a little humph, as if to say "Finally, I'm in the know." Immediately, he turned away and glided to the left towards the ticket counter that I was waiting to go up to. I watched closely as he simply walked past the counter and then made a U-turn, came out and walked back to the opposite side of the airport to rejoin the group, and where I could no longer see him. That was that. I had no idea why he had asked, I had no idea why he walked up that way and then turned around, I simply continued waiting my time.

Eventually I made it to the counter, bought the cheapest ticket I possibly could and then rejoined the others. Everyone was starting towards the cafeteria to get something to eat before the planes took off, so I joined them. There were about four of us eating together lovingly sharing reminiscences from the trip. When we were almost finished, one man looked at his watch and said that we'd better get going as it was near boarding time and the seats were first come first serve. I was familiar with what he was saying, as when I flew in from the states my seat was also first come first serve, but I said to him, "You know I think when I got my ticket I saw a seat number on it." He replied, "No, it's first, come first serve, you'd better get going." I took my time, finished my food and then got up to join the crowd ready to board. As I was standing in line, I thought I'd better check my ticket, so I pulled out my boarding pass and saw that there was in fact a seat number on it. I thought I had been right in remembering that. However, it wasn't until I was about to step into the plane that I realized the seat number I had seen was seat 3B. At once my brain began to compute that in *every* other flight in which I had flown in all of my years, seat "3 Anything" would be in First Class. At that moment I looked up and who was sitting in seats 4B and 4A, but the guru and his sister respectively. He didn't even look up; I simply took a few steps and fell into my seat directly in front of him, my heart fluttering in utter amazement. "What had he done!!??", I thought.

When I sat there trying to begin to understand and at the same time trying to compose myself being less than a foot in front of him, my attention was distracted as I noticed that other passengers continued to file into the plane, one in particular. The president of the organization, who when boarding saw me sitting in First Class in front of the guru and I could tell just decided that he would just sit down in First Class as well. He took a seat in the first row on the opposite side of the aisle. Then a few passengers later, another one of the guru's top teacher's saw me sitting, and he too took a seat in this section on the same side as the other one, but closer to me. Finally, an Indian woman who I had become friends with in Montreal and who often cooked for the guru boarded, and I grabbed her hand as she walked by and invited her to sit inside next to me by the window. I got up and she joined me in this third row. At about this time, one of the stewardesses came on board and noticed all of the passengers now seated in First Class. Looking quite surprised she began to ask each one for their boarding pass. First, she went to the president, she looked at his pass, and he immediately got up and went back into Coach. Next she went to the other teacher who had chosen to sit down across from me and he too was ousted. My Indian friend sitting beside me was stirring in her seat and was about to get up, but I slowly placed my hand on top of hers, settling her back into her seat. When the flight attendant came to me, and I handed her my boarding pass with the correct seat assignment on it, she simply said "Thank you." and the search ended. My seatmate sighed with relief, and we all settled in. I was stymied, could not speak one word, but knew that somehow, he had magically and lovingly arranged this. My friend reached back, handed the guru a section of her newspaper and we took off.

Our final tour stop was Maui. As soon as we landed, the guru was whisked away and taken to his hotel. We all quickly followed, and got to go inside his suite for a little while, but did not meet with him. Someone said that we would go on a tour with him a little later in the day, so I went and found a very inexpensive room at a hotel a few blocks away. It was close enough that I could see his hotel from my window. The room was cheap and I felt sad moving into it, but at least I was here in Hawaii and not far from him. As some time had gone by, I thought I should call the suite to see what time to be back for the tour. So I telephoned, expecting to speak with one of those attending him in the waiting room, but when the phone was picked up who answered but he. It was one of the first times that I had actually spoken to him on the phone. In his sweet voice, he told me to tell everyone that we would be leaving at 11a.m. and then quickly said good-bye. I got a chance to say nothing. I contacted a few people and they were all, including his top teachers, surprised that I was telling them when we were leaving and that I had spoken with him. Then and there, I decided I was finally going to tell him in person that I was now ready to be his. I loved him and needed him so much and I could not let my internal fears and inhibitions keep me from revealing my heart. In our psychic conversations, we had discussed this on many occasions, but in reality I felt as if I was never ready to stand up and *be* his. But now after the flight and the phone, I just said to myself and to him, internally, "It is time, I'm going to make it known to you as soon as I see you!"

I tried to rest, but could not; eventually I got dressed and walked the few blocks to his hotel. As I was entering the lobby, I heard someone call out my name, and I looked around and a woman said, "We are all outside in the cars waiting for You!" I was surprised, as I had gotten there a little before the time that he had said. I followed her outside and to my amazement there were four cars lined up at the curb, someone motioned me to the last car and said, "Here get in!" His car was at the front of the line. I was in the rear car. Another passenger in the car said to me, "You sure should feel special, because the guru refused to leave without you." But I was only feeling disappointment, because I had been certain that this was the time that I would profess my love and that we would be together, and yet again, disappointment.

Feeling dejected I tried to at least enjoy the tour. Local devotees were leading the caravan taking us to special sites to see. After driving and driving, trying to find the right spot, finally we stopped at one location where we had to walk some distance to even get to it. When we finally got to it, the guru walked out to the farthest rock appearing to be almost on the ocean and everyone gasped as a big wave crashed on the rocks and soaked him thru and thru. We then decided to go back to the cars, as there was a chill in the air. As I sat back in my seat waiting to take off, someone knocked at the car door where I was sitting. I opened it and it was a woman dressed in a saree; she had been riding with the guru. She said to me, "The guru said that you must think we are all nuts, all that walking back and forth, he said for you to trade places with me." And just like that, I was finally, and without pushing like all the other women did, in his car.

There were two others in the back seat, next to me in the middle was the handsome head teacher who had scolded me at the apartment; and on the other side of him was the woman who I had helped to go and speak with him. And even though I did not like that she was still riding with him, it did not matter; they were both irrelevant. *He* had *asked me* to get into his car. And I knew that he cared. I immediately hunched forward and put my hand on his shoulder; letting him know that I was happy that he brought me to him and that I loved him. I did not care that people rarely touched him, I did and he didn't move. Of course, the other woman, seeing that I had my hand on him, immediately then put her hand on his other shoulder as we returned to the hotel. Many times, others upon seeing our interactions, tried to copy what was very natural and right between us and sometimes it appeared true; but the energy between us was authentic and people knew.

Somewhere during this trip the guru took a very small group, maybe eight or ten of us with him to attend a meeting he was having with a Hindu Spiritual leader, who was the founder of a large Hindu newspaper. I was surprised, as this man turned out to be a white, and I assumed to be American. He had a long grayish beard and was dressed in orange robes, huge Rudraksha beads (prayer beads) around his neck, and long dreadlocks: and obviously quite important. While the two men met, the rest of us sat across from them a few feet away facing them. As I sat, and looked at the man, I became aware of energy coming fully in me; so much so that I felt as if I was in a full meditation, but with my eyes wide open. The more that my eyes fixated on him, I began to notice his face becoming blurry; so much so that it began to change shape, and before my eyes, he was now bald and clean-shaven. I was somewhat surprised, but it had happened once before and what I realized in the moment was that this was his past life revealing itself to me. No sooner did I have this comprehension than I heard him say to the guru, "You brought a lot of power with you today." I knew that he knew who I was.....

Even with all of the miraculous happenings on this trip, it still ended badly with yet another unfulfilled connection. Out of money, and fearful because for some reason my ATM cards would not work, I went to one of his teachers who I knew had money to ask if I could borrow some funds to help me to get back to the states. He looked at me, put his hands in his pockets and turned them inside out and said that the guru's sister had hit him up for an orphanage in India and he had nothing. I cried. Extremely worried, later I went to the room of the owner of the first home that we had stayed with; crying, I shared what had happened and he lovingly handed me $100. The final night I was so angered by all that had transpired, the fact that I was in a cheap hotel and right across the street was the 5-star hotel he was in, and the absolute wrongness of this situation. I resolved to release him and this mistreatment. I regained my strength. Feeling empowered I went to sleep, got up, packed, and got on the plane to return home. While sitting in my seat, I was feeling like myself for the first time in a long time. A man who I had never before seen, sat down next to me and said, "Aren't you with Sri Ravi Shankar?" and once again, he came into me from afar, and my heart succumbed.

Chapter Thirteen
I Love You Too

A few days after arriving back to Los Angeles he continued his Western States tour with an evening public appearance in Los Angeles. I had been the person who arranged this talk, prior to going to Hawaii and had secured a beautiful, large and well-known church in Westwood for the venue. A year before I had organized the event for him in the Black Community and I had also brought him to UCLA to speak at the Religious Studies Department, while I was still in my doctoral program; it had been his first visit to the University. In this one I did not have a major a role, but since I had been the person who found the location, I had signed the contract and was responsible for making sure that we fulfilled our end of the agreement.

The day of the talk, I went to speak to him to go over details of the evening. He was staying with the devotee, who I had initially traveled to India with, and whose house he always stayed in. In fact, she kept a bedroom just for his once or twice a year visits. I was allowed into his room to meet with him. It was one of very few times that we were actually allowed to be alone together. (*In fact later I was told that the organization had held a meeting to figure out how we could be kept apart.*) What could anyone say? I had organized the event and had to meet with him prior to it. I entered his room and immediately his jet-black endless eyes starred at me. Those Indian eyes that always look as if he had applied make-up, perfectly, stared right thru me. He was walking around the room getting ready for the evening, but still in his robes and a beige wool wrap from the afternoon Satsang he had given earlier in the day. He told me to have a seat, and so, I sat down on his bed (as there really was nowhere else to sit), as he moved back and forth across the small room. I began going over the details, telling him what the church was like and the timing of the activities and told him that I would be driving him to and from the event. He agreed. And, then, when I had run out of things to say, I remember my head kind of hanging down as I began to speak, to speak the words I had never said to anyone in this entire lifetime. I had been holding my life tight inside of me for far too long. Finally I had to let them out, they were my life, - "You know, like all the other women in the organization, I. HAVE FALLEN...COMPLETELY... IN LOVE... WITH... YOU...". And, without a second's hesitation, he interrupted my stuttering, took his bottled water away from his lips in mid-air. The room stood still, long enough for him to bring my lowered head to attention. He stopped everything, including the drink he was drinking and looked me directly in the eyes and said, "Me Too......"

My heart stopped, it was as if nothing else existed; nothing else but those eyes, the eyes of god. Not the spiritual god, but the god of my world, the man of my life, looking at me with every ounce of seriousness that his infinitely strong being could hold. Telling me his absolute truth.

And yet still, I had not grown into my womanhood enough to fully grasp the true meaning of what he was saying, what he was doing: revealing to me his all. The words that I have never heard that he had said to anyone.........

Gently, he broke the absolute silence in the air by asking me, "Is this okay to wear tonight?" referring to the outfit that he was still wearing from earlier. I stumbled and replied something like, "Well if you put on a nicer shawl," actually expecting that he was going to change into something more ornate for the evening's event; but truly unable to think at all. The energy in the air was so intense. Immediately without a knock, the door opened and it was the owner of the house. I saw that she perceived the intensity of the energy present between us and that she was glad that she had in fact broken into it. She told him that he had a telephone call from the venue, and handed the phone to him. He took it, and I could tell that the person on the other end asked him a question; which he then deferred to me. I told him that there was no need to do whatever it was, and he replied on the phone, then again another question and he almost turned to me again; but he looked up at the woman whose face showed her dislike for him asking me, and he just answered on his own.

And of course, then it was time to leave. There was no time to even consider taking in what had just happened between us. The car piled up with devotees and we were off. I did get to escort him to the church steps and when we arrived, the owner of the house with a group of other ladies approached us. This woman, who even in her 60's, immediately came up to him, with flowers in hand, and a girlish smile that I had never seen on her before and said to him "Tonight, you're coming home with me! humph" He immediately turned and looked at me presumably because we had already made our arrangements, but I wasn't completely present, and said nothing.

The evening was beautiful. He looked magnificent with the grandiose cathedral altar as a backdrop. The music was wonderful as always and the audience filling the room to the brim seemed to truly enjoy it. At the end, he stood at the center of the pulpit and decided to give darshan, hugging each and every person present, one-by-one. I thought he may not be aware that the time was getting on and that the contract that we had signed said that we must vacate by a certain hour. Very much in my administrative mode, I went to him, whispered in his ear that we needed to wrap up as we had to clean the hall after everyone had vacated. Within a short time, he ended the ceremony, and I assume walked out of the cathedral. I of course, was focused on clearing things up and getting us out of the building on time. I had completely forgotten our discussion of my driving him home and the interaction with the other woman or of our extraordinary exchange that day. All I was concerned about was clearing up the flowers, getting the electricity out, putting the altar back in place and leaving the venue as good as or better than we had found it (something the guru had taught us over the years.)

When things were completed, I walked to my car, alone, and then returned to the house where he was staying. There was a lot of hustle bustle happening, I inquired as to what was going on and was told that the guru had at the last minute decided to pack and head on up to Santa Barbara that night. So everyone was frantically gathering their things in order to accompany him. I was surprised as his venue was not until the following afternoon and I had thought he was leaving in the morning.

Somewhat hesitant, I made my way into his room and asked him if it was okay if I came to Santa Barbara. Head down, seeming quite busy packing his infamous "black bag", he looked up at me and in an extremely brusque voice, retorted, "If you have the time!" I was taken aback, ignorant and confused by his abrupt and angry tone.

The next day, I drove to Santa Barbara and rejoined the entourage at the home of the President of the organization. The house was full of devotees scattered around reading and talking. I went into the kitchen to find a L.A. devotee cooking in the kitchen. This woman was quite pushy, always feeling and acting like she thought she should be in charge. When I asked her where he was, she told me he was upstairs meeting with some top teachers. I then turned and went towards the stairs. I heard her yell out behind me, "You can't go up there!" in her terse rough voice. But after the prior day's events, I didn't care what she said. Straightaway I made my way to the staircase and went up. When I got to the door, it was closed, and so I knocked. His top teacher, a beautiful Indian-American woman, who I knew well, opened the door. She told me they were in a meeting, but to wait. Just a few moments later, the door opened and she let me in. The moment I stepped in, she, stepped out. This moment was very important to me, as it was obvious to me, that even though I knew that this teacher, like most of his other teachers and devotees, did not want us together; she was the only one, who appeared to put his wishes above her own, and graciously made a way for us to be together alone. He lovingly smiled and greeted me, as she closed the door and left. As the door was closing, I could hear the very loud-mouthed teacher from the kitchen screaming, "She's not supposed to be up there!" He continued around the room and was just beginning a light conversation, when the door burst open, and in walked a male teacher who was very big in the organization, a small built, but very aggressive man. He immediately plopped down, crossed his arms and stared at the guru. The guru paused, turned to me and told me to go downstairs and join the others and that he would be down soon. Never feeling confident enough about my position with him, I let go, obeyed his direct request and went downstairs, no idea about what had just occurred.

Chapter Fourteen
The Trees

That next fall there was a course at the Montreal Ashram in less than a week. I had only a small amount of money and was staying with a good friend in Santa Monica doing Temporary Work, which I often did in between travels; but at that time, mostly all I had was *longing*.

He was very much "with me" - Adoring me, loving me, bringing me to ecstasy. And because of his continuous pleasures, I felt absolutely certain that I should be with him at the Course. The *calling* from within was telling me to Come. Over and over he made me know that he wanted me. And so, I decided to step outside my lonely *inner knowingness* into the outer "real world". If, it was truly Him, and he loved me and wanted me the way that I wanted him, then He would bring me to him. He would support me in the external world. He would verify my inner knowingness. And so, with my heart in my hands, I sent him an e-mail, saying that I heard his call, and that Yes, I truly wanted to be *with* him, in heart, in mind and in body, *and* that I needed his help on the earthly plane in order to get there. I told him, "I am yours and you are mine and if you want me to be with you, I know you have the power to get me there."

What I needed to actually get there was both the course fee (which included accommodations and food) and the airfare. With trepidation, I sent off the e-mail and within moments, I got the idea to call the ashram and offer to do my energy healing work for donations to the ashram in exchange for my course fees. And astonishingly within less than an hour, I got an e-mail back saying YES, come and do your work, you are welcome!

I was overjoyed, amazed, astonished. Was he showing me that he *really did* want me there with him? My heart began to move from the state of continuous doubt to the possibility of it all: the confirmation of my knowing and affirmation of my intense love.

However, there was still the plane fare. I had only about $300 and flights to Montreal were $450 to $500. I wasn't sure what to do, and immediately it occurred to me to ask my lovely friend who I was staying with, who had traveled extensively for her profession, if she had any miles that she would be willing to sell to me for $250. She stopped only for a moment and said, "Well as a matter of fact, I do. I have miles in a few accounts, and most have to be transferred; but in my American Express account I think I have just enough to get you a ticket and it could be done immediately." She got on the phone and within a half an hour, the ticket in my name was completed.

The excitement within my being was sooo strong, a deep deep stirring of what had been suppressed for so long. A disbelief and yet at the same time the beginnings of a belief. I had never put him to the test, I never spoke out and said *help* me. I thought it was all up to me. And now, I was coming out of my shell and moving towards the light; moving towards him. I would not be afraid of anything any longer. I would just go forth. By providing the means, he had proven to me that he did want me, and I was going to give him my all. No more holding back.

A few days later I was on the plane, barely breathing. Unable to comprehend all that was occurring. It was heaven. A feeling I was not used to having. For so many years there had been this overriding doubt, not being able to fully comprehend what was actually happening. Was he communicating with me? Does he truly love me? Are these things that are going on inside of me truly real? Could I be creating all of it? I had always been such a logical being; a Ph.D. will do that. That was all I knew. I knew that these things that had taken me over all of these years were new, that nothing like this had ever happened inside or outside of me like this, and yet I had to always question, because, he did not operate like most men that I knew. He did not come right out and say I want you, I love you. Well, yes, he did say it that one time, in Los Angeles that past spring, but there was always hesitancy afterwards; always this uncomfortable space, which never seemed to get filled or completed. There was always this looming doubt in my mind and heart; and so, fear took over – Always. But NOW, I had the proof. I asked in the world and he answered. True, it was not his words coming out of his mouth. True he did not hand me the ticket to come, but this is who *he* is. *He* is not like other men, this is how *he* works. And I knew that. The Indian women always knew it and so did his long-time followers. He makes all things happen from within out. And, the *out* did occur. I *was* on a plane, I *was* on my way to be with him and it was a direct response to my asking.

I arrived in Montreal and took a taxi to the familiar bus terminal, which would take me out to the ashram or to the town from which we were picked up. I purchased my ticket and then went across the street to a shopping mall nearby where I would wait until time for the bus. The shopping center was beautiful, quite modern, a cross between a typical U.S. mall and yet something completely different. One of a kind shops, a unique feel, not a carbon copy of every mall in the states, only the external feel of a familiar indoor mall. In the center was a stage and this time there was music playing- jazz, and the center court was filled with people during their lunchtime enjoying the jam. The food court was on the side of this center area and I decided to have lunch while waiting for the bus, but as the music was happening, I decided to stand and enjoy it for awhile before eating. It was fabulous, absolutely captivating taking me over with its trance like rhythms. Not a big jazz lover myself, I was well aware of how much enjoyment this song was giving me, a cross between Latin and jazz. When it was over, the crowd applauded as the bandleader took the mike. Still impacted by the music, I was taken aback when he shared in his soothing sexy voice that the name of that piece was "Seduction". At once, I realized that that is what these past few months had been. All of the internal loving messages, all of the ecstatic moments, all of the magic.

And it was right; I had been completely seduced into coming back to him. I had never ever known the true meaning of that word.

No man had ever really seduced me. One of those many words, that until you have the experience of it, is just another combination of alphabets in the language; one for which you think you have an idea, but in reality, not. No true meaning. But now I knew. He had seduced me from the inside out. This is where I was.

I sat and had my lunch and relished in the feeling of warmth that poured through me; a feeling of love and desire growing and being fed with every moment. Peace, utter letting go into the waves of emotions, which had long before swept through my being, but to which I always held myself at bay; releasing into the depths of their arms, relaxing into trust - Letting go.

After sometime, I loaded onto the bus and eventually arrived at my destination, Trois Rivieres, and a car from the ashram was there to pick me up. By the time I arrived it was late. When I checked in at the front desk, Satsang was already over. I was informed that the first Course was ending that night and that course attendees would be leaving in the morning, with the next course beginning tomorrow. Because of that, there was only a space for me in a cabin with bunks. I was disappointed as I wanted to have my own space. I asked if I could stay in the healing room, in which I would be working. They told me that was okay for that night only and that they would try to find another space for me in the morning. I went to the room, put my things down under the massage table said a prayer, brushed my teeth and immediately went to his house.

Looking back, I was amazed that after all the times I had been there before, all the hurt, all the rejections, all the remembrances of being turned away at his door resulting in my inability to act spontaneously and the crushing of my heart, all of those memories were gone. They were long forgotten in the Now of *that* moment; a newfound sense of surety that had been lost in my being, a confidence, an absoluteness that guided my every step. I went to the door, knocked, it opened, and I walked right in past whoever had answered it; oblivious to their being, utterly confident in the rightness of my movements.

I entered the living room and there he was sitting in his chair, I ran to him, fell to the floor in front of him and took his hand - a very first. He looked at me, greeted me and in no way moved my hand away from his. He allowed me to continue holding it as I collapsed at his feet in my longing, in my love. I could vaguely feel the presence of others, it seemed like mostly women - five or six. But truly, I was unaware of them.

Whatever else he had been doing stopped. He looked directly into my eyes and in a deep voice asked me when I had arrived. I told him I had only just come. He asked me how my trip was and I replied that it was fine. Suddenly, I became aware of a stiffness in him. Even though he was speaking, he did not move, there appeared to be an internal armor around his being, which felt extremely uncomfortable. It was as if he could not move. At the same time, I did become aware of the people surrounding us, in particular one of his top teachers (the one to whom I had previously confided my anger with him and the intimacies which had occurred between us). She stood there above me in shock as I lay before him exposed in my love. And then, as if he were a stuffed animal head bolted on a wall, hanging for all to stare at, he said, "Go take a shower" (words which later I wish I had taken literally). The words hung in the air, just as still as the eyes which were pouring down on us from all of the women, and most especially from that one woman. My head began to lift as if coming up from out of a fog. What did he say? " Go take a shower?????" " Am I hearing things?????" As I lifted my eyes in disbelief, there he sat, staring at me, repeating his words. And as my mind attempted to comprehend them, they hit my heart like a dagger, as well as being helped along by the woman saying, "Kamala, he wants you to go". I stood up, in shock, frozen in disbelief, turned away, and walked out the door, utterly and completely dejected. My Being unable to rectify the seeming rejection, which had just occurred, with the built up feelings of love, which had begun living in me for the past week. I fell into absolute and complete devastation.

In a dreamlike state, I found my way in the dark through the ashram forest, back to the office, went in and asked what time the first shuttle was going to the airport in the morning. They told me it was at 5am. I informed them that I would not be staying for the course and that they should reserve a space for me in the morning car. I went back to the healing room, opened up my sleeping bag and lay down fully clothed and dissolved.

The next morning I woke up changed, distanced from the numbness of the night before, the reality of what I thought had occurred stirred in my being, I then concluded, that in fact, he did not want me, and that what I had thought all along was false. All I could feel was relief that at last I had clarity. It was enough. I got up, packed up the few items that I had taken out, went to the entrance and stepped into the car going back to the airport. There were three other passengers; I loaded in with a woman and a man in the back; a fourth person was in the front with the driver.

As I sat silent, still unable to comprehend, or even be in a place to consider understanding what had occurred, they chattered about how wonderful the course had been. How fast the week had gone by and how happy they were to have been there. Eventually, the woman next to me, a head teacher, turned to me and asked how the course had been for me. I told her, "I did not do the course." She replied, "What?" I explained that I had come that night, I saw the guru, and that I got what I needed and that I was going home. She paused, thought, and then said to me – "Does the guru know you are going back?" I said "No." She paused again, this time a little longer and finally said, "I *really* think that you should go back and let him know. He rarely advises running away from things."

Her words stung in my ear. Above all else, I knew that I had to release patterns, which no longer served me. I knew that I had an ancient habit of running away from things. I knew that it was finally time to drop this way of dealing with difficulties. I looked at her and admitted that running away was not something that I admired in myself. I, in no way, felt that he was worth returning to. I felt that I had gotten clarity on that, but I truly wanted to break the habit of *fight or flight*. And so, after a few moments of thought and with resolve, I chose to return in the car to the ashram, to face him, to face my fears and pains and to release a longstanding unhealthy pattern.

After going to the airport, staying for awhile to pick up the next group, by the time we arrived back at the ashram, it was time for mid-morning Satsang. I checked into my room and went immediately to the hall to face him.

Once seated, however, the site of him made me ill. I was enraged. There was nothing of me that could look at him. Filled with anger of his seeming rejection of my affection, I was unable to stay in Satsang with him and the three hundred others. I walked out! Out beyond the building, out into the woods. Walking, walking, walking, to get away. On one level I was present and aware, and yet on another needing a container for my immense feelings of hurt, distrust and betrayal as a result of his words. Only the sky and the earth were large enough to enclose their immensity.

I continued on in furor, horror and sadness. How could he have made a way, allowed me to come, internally loved me so much and yet when I came with all my love and courage up, he dismissed me – in a second!

After awhile, little by little, my mind began to settle as the hurt began to drain through my body, out down through my feet, down into the earth. Each step loosening the tightness in my mind, the hate, the hurt, going down through my legs into the floor of those magnificent woods. Each leaf that I stepped on grabbing my rage, the Mother in all her glory doing Her work of healing. Until finally, I was free. Free from the pain. Free from the hurt. Free under the skies, free over the rocks, free under the trees. Everything completely released from my being; the moments before no longer existing, only the Now. My pace began to slow and finally I stopped, into the complete stillness of my surround. The great beauty of the forest, which surrounded me took me into Her.

In motionless movement, my eyes gradually lifted to the wonders that lay before them. The trees, which I had walked in and seen many many times, the trees which had been there all along, the trees which had surrounded me on another magical day, in which a butterfly had landed on my arm and rested for over a half an hour. But now, on this day, the trees revealed to me what my former eyes had never seen, had never known, had never imagined - the unseen. For before me they revealed in their trunks, in their leaves, in their branches, the truth of their being – that they were in fact completely and fully vibrational. Like brown and green and orange water, hanging in the air, absolutely fluid, I knew that if I raised my hand, which I of course knew not to do, I would have swam right through them.

Again seemingly motionless, my eyes moved slowly down to my body, I saw my hands which were now also wholly vibrational as well – floating, fluid, translucent hands.

Simultaneously, I became aware that the actual space between me and the trees, the very air that I breathed was itself a river connecting me and them, and in that moment, I understood that in actuality there was no me and them. We were utterly and completely ONE. One world, one body, one mind, with no disconnect, fluid, lucid, oneness.

(e-mail)
My Dearest,

As I sit here, questioning everything, wanting to Be and Love my Godself Only, I do long for someone to talk to. But who can I talk to about this stuff of God. I find I can no longer talk to you inside, my best friend and companion, you who are al. When I do, inside I know I am speaking to the Universe and you at once, and of course to Myself. But it is nice to have a cup of tea and chat with another human being, about the things in my heart and mind. But who can understand my thoughts and choices in living. So I am writing you. I get angry and say, why can't you call me back, why can't you respond to me. You are a man and God - CALL ME. But it doesn't seem to help. You who have shown me that you love me, yet I still always question. What used to be God's way, seems only to be My way now. But Jesus did speak to the Father above (indicating both He and It), so I know that there is something more and I AM that as well. It's still difficult for me. Do I keep loving you and wanting you as mine, expecting that God would not give you to me and love me and make me feel that you were mine if you can't be. Or do I look at my life and say- new choices are necessary. I am grateful for having had it inside - I am. I have always loved God and my love knows no end for the love that I have experienced internally with you. I know how much God loves me to have given me that. AND, I still want it all.

Chapter Fifteen
He's Sick

The course had come to an end. This time, he and the four hundred or so attendees were headed to a talk in a nearby city. Everyone had already left the ashram to be on time for the event, but for some reason I did not have a ride. This was unusual, and so I just let it be, not knowing why, but just conscious that there must be some reason. However, once again, the feeling of being unrequited, unsatisfied, incomplete was very much with me. How many more times would I have to go through this push pull, love and let go? When will he ever consummate this energy and knowingness inside me? How can he keep turning it on and off? I was so angry and frustrated; I went to his house on the last day, just to try once again to connect with him.

As I walked up to the entryway, and stepped inside the atrium/ reception area, I was uncomfortable as always, afraid yet again that I would be turned away. But, I was too filled with anger to stop. I went to the door and knocked, and after a few moments the male head teacher who was on the Board of Directors and often planned things for him, who had come into the room between us in Santa Barbara and who I often felt did not care for me at all, opened the door. I asked, "Can I see the guru before he leaves for the talk?" He replied curtly and matter-of-factly, "The guru is sick and won't be going to the talk. He will come out later on." Not waiting for a response from me, he stuck his head back inside and closed the door. I was livid! He, is

NEVER sick! I did not believe one word he was saying. I thought he was covering for the guru and that he would sneak out the back door of the house without acknowledging or saying good-bye to me. I was so angry that I refused to move from the seat in front of his door. I just sat there. A half an hour or more went by and finally that teacher came back out, but this time with his coat and bags. He told me that the guru would come out for Satsang that evening. And then he walked out of the atrium with bags in hand. I was surprised, and somewhat in disbelief, but was beginning to think perhaps there was a reason that I was one of the few people who did not have a ride to the town and was left on site with the guru.

Evening came and there was in fact a Satsang. Our small group perhaps 15-25 which included the ashram staff, were quite happy when he came in and to be there, so close with him, even though he was "sick". He came and simply had a conversation with us, and coughed occasionally. He spoke a little slower than normal, but all in all did not seem too bad off. Afterwards we walked him to his house and I asked him if there was anything that I could do for him. He told me to come tomorrow that I could help him, it appeared that he was alone and that there was no one there helping him. When I got there the next morning, he answered the door, but inside, was a guy I had seen before at a course somewhere. We had a positive relationship, but had met only that one time. He was very unlike the people who usually cared for the guru. Real working class type in jeans and a sweater, and looked kind of tired and unresponsive.

I asked the guru what I could do for him. Suddenly the guy looked up and realized that he should get up and take care of things. The guru then led him into the kitchen and showed him a pile of dirt and dust that he swept but was behind the broom. Since I had previously cleaned the house, for the first time, I felt extremely comfortable taking an authoritative role and telling them both to get out of the kitchen that I could take care of that! Both the guy and the guru looked up at me, and the guru just took him and walked away, indicating that it was okay for me to do the job. Given that okay, I proceeded to be at home, cleaning the kitchen and feeling quite comfortable. That afternoon when it was time to think about dinner, I asked him if I could fix dinner for him. He told me to go rest for awhile and then go to the kitchen and get a few items. Following his words, I rested, quite happy about finally having some precious time with him. When I returned with my packages in hand, to my surprise, there was an older ashram female resident, seated in the living room with the man, and I did not see the guru. And then to my surprise, he popped out of the kitchen, looked at me, with two plates of food in his hand, placed one on the table and said, "Here, this is for you!" and then took the other plate and proceeded to walk upstairs to his rooms. Everyone was startled, I was both surprised and bowled over with affection, as he had sent me to get food when in actuality *he* had wanted and planned to fix dinner for *me*. It reminded me that even internally, he often had a kind and fun and surprising way of making me happy. As he climbed the spiral staircase, I thought I heard him say under his breath, "come upstairs", but I was so shocked by what had occurred, that I thought it was only an internal message in my mind, not in the room for others to hear and I was much too timid to proceed up after him.

The following day his manservant and I were in and out of his house, taking care of his needs. When afternoon came, he told us he was going upstairs for a rest. And so we both knew that it was fine to just sit in his house and be in peace/heaven. I had forgotten these sweet moments where I did not have to fight to be with him and to completely let go in his space, however it was only short lived. He had been upstairs for only about ten minutes when the phone rang. There was one right next to where I was sitting and one upstairs in his room as he answered it and we could hear him talking. Ten minutes later the phone rang again, and I was hesitant to answer it, but was concerned that he would not be able to take his rest. So when I heard him hang up, I decided to go upstairs and ask him if he would like for me to take the calls downstairs and give him messages after his nap. I got up from my seat, walked across the room and began to ascend the narrow spiral staircase. No sooner did my foot take the first step up, did the front door open, which was only two feet from the staircase where I was; and in walked the co-manager/husband of the ashram. Immediately he shouted at me with a great force, "DON'T YOU GO UP THERE!!!" The impact of his shout shook my entire being and reverberated through my heart. Stunned, but aware, as we both simultaneously turned and looked up, and standing just a few steps above me descending from the next turn of the staircase was the guru perceiving ALL that had occurred.

I remember very little after that except feeling as if I had been bludgeoned. I believe the guru told me to go and have dinner and the next thing I remember is sitting in the dining room hall at the table; dazed and out of my body and out of my mind. There were only a few of us at the ashram and I think there were about ten or so at the table. And, eventually that man joined the table. I tried to sit and eat, but I could not. It made me sick to be anywhere near him

Somebody/something, guru,/god/self, sensing that I was out of control, out of my senses, picked my body up and took me outside. And *it* walked me and walked me and walked me. Not aimlessly, but specifically, out into the woods and around a particular path, up the hill; purposely and forcefully. I had no idea where I was headed, but I was too out of my being to care.

Up a steep hill, past a no trespassing sign, *it* maintained a steady and fervent pace that my heart and limbs could endure, but barely.... Until finally at the precipice, it stopped, turned my body and instantly revealed to my eyes the most beautiful endless sky at just the beginnings of sunset. A sky so exquisite, so vast with blues and oranges, that I *knew* that all of my hurt, pain, fear, and anger would dissolve into it, be washed away by it, melted, vanquished, in all its glory. And IT, whatever it was, wanted me *to know* it, that there was a healing place for me and that I was not alone.

I learned in that moment what Maya Angelou meant in her poem- A Rock, A River, A Tree:

> "...*The rock cries out today, you may stand on me, But do not hide your face Across the wall of the world, A river sings a beautiful song, Come rest here by my side. Each of you a bordered country, Delicate and strangely made proud, Yet thrusting perpetually under siege. Your armed struggles for profit Have left collars of waste upon My shore, currents of debris upon my breast. Yet, today I call you to my riverside, If you will study war no more. Come, clad in peace and I will sing the songs The Creator gave to me when I And the tree and stone were one...*"

This healing sky, the healing of nature, thank God that it knew the depths of our cruelty to one another, the immensity of our envy, the enormity of our arrogance and pride. And it gave us/me Itself, to heal.

That evening, emotionally healed, after Satsang, he told me to come back early the next morning (the day he was to leave). I arrived at his door at 8:00am. He opened the door himself, let me in, and I sat down. He was alone, and told me he was about to have a meeting and to just stay seated on the side of the room where I was. Within moments a few of the ashram staff, upper management, including the man who had screamed at me, entered the house. With me sitting over to the left of them, he proceeded to meet with them and go over the budget for the next six months. They reported to him how much money had been made on the course, what their current bills were and estimated expenses. Within moments he brilliantly calculated how much they would need for the next few months and decided that they were okay for awhile. It was amazing to watch his mind work, well ahead of the rest who knew the figures, but he could calculate all in a moment. Once he had settled things, others began to come in, until the full ashram staff of twelve or so were present in the room seated before him. After a bit, he rose and went into the kitchen. And then in front of everyone, he called me into the kitchen and handed me his dishes and a special silk bag that they were kept in and told me to put them inside and then put them in the car. After I had followed his orders (a bit disheveled as I had never been asked to do anything personal for him before), I returned into the room. He then came to me with a large container of powdered herbal greens and a smaller one. He told me, again in front of everyone, to fill the smaller container, and the other container was for ME and pushed them into my hands. And, he said, when you finish, go upstairs and put them in my suitcase. I went into the kitchen and nervously filled the container, still not understanding what was going on. And then in front of all of his staff, including the man who had screamed at me the day before, I ascended the spiral staircase and went into his room. I had not been there since years before at my very first visit to that ashram when I had been assigned the task of cleaning his house.

By then, he had already gone upstairs and told me where to place them. I looked around the room and asked him was there anything else that I could do for him. The only thing in the room was his one suitcase. He instructed me to go and tell the man who had hurt me, to come upstairs and to bring his suitcase down. In that very moment, I realized the power of his love, the masterfulness of his actions, and his absolute care for all. As I glided down the stairs, I realized that I was given the opportunity not only to show everyone including that cruel man, that he did in fact love me, but *I* was also being given the gift of telling *him* that the guru needed him and that *he too* could go up the stairs into his room. It was perfection in action. He had taken care of every detail of my heart and of the lessons to be learned. My heart praised him.

When the then humbled man had brought down the bag and walked it out to the car, I knew that everything in the room had been cleared, however, when I heard him flush the toilet upstairs, I decided on my own to walk up the stairs one last time, just to show and hold onto this power that I had been given. When I entered the room, the guru stood in the center of the room looking at me, then his eyes diverted down towards his feet, and there laying in front of him on the floor, folded neatly was a white sheet that had not been there before.

Chapter Sixteen
Amma

While back in California, it was during this very intense year that I had two beautiful spiritual communications with the guru's Mother. About April or May of that year, I was in Los Angeles, staying at one of my many residents during that time, when one evening while meditating; a very deep energy came over me. And a voice, not like the voice that usually communed with me, it was a bit higher and closer to *his* actual voice. It said, "My lovely Mother would like to speak with you….." And then, a beautiful energy came into my consciousness and we meditated for awhile and eventually it spoke, "You won't get back to India before I leave my body." I was taken aback…so wonderfully filled with the ecstasy and remarkableness of this communion, and yet at the same time so surprised by the words. I can remember coming out of it to think enough to respond back and quickly, "then I can come NOW." And with that, the beautiful energy slowly faded away, and I was left in a state of deep love, peace and wonder.

I remembered our brief encounter at the Indian Ashram, when she anonymously came up to me and took my nametag in her hand. I sat thinking what all she might have actually known in that brief moment.

Six months later, a very similar experience occurred in which in meditation, his voice came to me again, with the exact same words,

"My lovely Mother would like to speak with you.", but this time, there were no words from her. It was simply an extraordinary depth and beauty of communion. I felt an energy so present with me and not words, but the feeling associated with it was that I was his wife and that I would care for him. It was sooo lovely, this vibration, and it stayed in me for almost an hour, but eventually released. A week later, via the e-Satsang that we all received, there was a notification that the guru's mother was ill and had been taken to the hospital; and only one week later, that she had passed. During the six months prior, there had been no indication that she had ever been sick. I knew nothing of this, except that one message via the e-mail. A few months later in one of the few times that he spoke about his Mother publicly, he mentioned that the dying prepare six months in advance. When I calculated the number of months between the first communication that I had with her and her death, it was exactly six months. One of the next times that I saw him and spoke to him was in Singapore before his upcoming birthday in Jakarta, in our private conversation, he mentioned his mother to me. When I told someone about his words, even though at the time they did not seem significant to me, they remarked, "He spoke about his Mother to you? He hasn't spoken to anyone about her since her passing.

Chapter Seventeen
Surprise Trip to Gurupurnima

That spring, I was in California preparing for my daughter's graduation from high school. We moved in with a wealthy old friend whose wife had left him and who we kept company by staying in a wing of his house. After graduating, my daughter got a full-time job at the dance studio where she had been studying and teaching for years and I continued my work at the hospital, working with patients with more and more serious illnesses. The healings continued to be powerful and the kriyas (spontaneous yoga movements) had completely stopped.

The following month I received a surprise phone call from two male Indian students who I had taught the breath course to. They were interested in going to the Gurupurnima course in Lake Tahoe that month, but would only go if I would come with them. I resisted somewhat as I was getting tired of dealing with the organization and their pushing us apart. I told them that I did not have the money to get there or lodging. They told me that they were only going for the two-day celebration and promised that they would pick me up, drive me and pay for my lodging. How could I say no?

Much to my surprise, they picked me up in a Lincoln Town Car, put me in the back seat and escorted me in the six-hour drive, taking care of my every need. Much like Indian men, they kept the conversation mostly between themselves, but occasionally I got in a few sentences. We arrived at the course and went straight to the day-long program. When the big Satsang was over, the two men and I went to the guru's house to try to see him. When we got to his porch, it was very unusual to see only a few people gathered outside and that some of his very top and close teachers were standing *outside*. Usually there was a large crowd outside his door, and these people were *always* on the inside. I walked up to his door and knocked. A teacher answered and informed me that the guru was not seeing *anyone* and had informed *everyone* to go home. I had my two Indian male companions with me and as they were new to the program I asked her to inform him. She said okay and then closed the door.

As we waited outside, one of his head teachers who was standing on the porch approached me and asked who the gentlemen were. I informed her that they were new and had taken the course only recently. In a commanding voice, she said, "Oh, the guru will want to see them!" And then kind of grabbed their arms and took them to the door and knocked. When the person answered the door again, this teacher tried to push her way in with the Indian gentlemen, and the woman on the other side of the door said, "the guru will see Kamala and her two friends tomorrow. Everyone else go home."

The next morning we went to his house and I was quite surprised at how quiet it was. Not the usual hustle bustle of activity in his home. We found him seated on a chair in the first room. I turned around and noticed only two people, a man and woman, teachers that I knew, were in the kitchen with their backs to us. He kindly greeted the two gentlemen, speaking to them in Hindi and I assume welcoming them. After a short conversation, they got up and told me they were leaving and I said I would see them later as it was obvious he wanted to speak to me. When they had left, and only the couple was left in the kitchen, obviously trying to listen, he asked me, "so what is this talk about we are going to get married?" "You shouldn't say that." in a not very scolding voice (I realized that I had said to my one girlfriend that after the personal things which had occurred in Montreal, where he really showed me that he wanted me, that I felt that he was in fact going to marry me.) I sat there right beneath him looking up at him very upset and just started recounting to him all that had happened, reminding him of what he did in Montreal and everything else. He just kind of sat there and said nothing. Angry, frustrated, I finally started crying and just got up, and ran out the door.

When I went outside, I immediately ran into one of his teachers, a very distinguished and considerate man, who stands way above the crowd in comparison to his other teachers in terms of character. I had never spent much time with this man, but when he saw me crying, he came to me and asked me what was bothering me so. As I began to try to talk, I just kept crying and he said, 'Here here, let's go and sit and talk." We walked away from the house and found a quiet place in the beautiful nature of the grounds, and I began to calm myself enough to tell him what had just transpired and why it was all so upsetting to me. For the first time, I shared with someone all that had happened over the past two years. I shared the energies, I shared the internal dialogues, I shared the plane seats, I shared my healing abilities and I shared that he had told me he loved me. He attempted to console me and to correct me, but when I haphazardly mentioned that moment when we were alone in his room in Hawaii and that the guru touched my hair, he stopped and said, "He touched your hair?" He was almost startled. And I replied, "Yes?" as I didn't see anything big about that. And then, his entire demeanor changed. He became very quiet, and even introspective, and thought a long time before he responded. "You know, a lot of people will be *very* jealous, if they hear about all that you have been given." And then of course I began to share more and more and more, until it was all out of me. He just sat there quietly, listening, receiving and allowing me to calm down. I was so deeply grateful to him, as I had had no one to share these things with.

I remember later, calmer and yet so filled with rage, when my friend who occasionally let me know about things people were saying and doing about me saw me, and the look on my face, she assumed that I was hurt by what the guru might have said and wanted to comfort me. But she was wrong; I was absolutely and completely enraged by this godman, and his switching stories and actions. And so I went to the Indian men and just said, 'I don't want to stay for the course, I want to leave." And we left.

Chapter Eighteen
Germany

The guru always spent Christmas at the ashram in Germany. That year, I prayed and worked hard so that my daughter and I could go. Even though she didn't like to go with me to these spiritual courses, I talked her into it with the stipulation that she could be home to spend New Year's Eve with her friends. There was a continuation of the course in Italy for New Year's Eve, but I did not have the funds to attend it, so I had purchased her return ticket and left mine open just in case a miracle happened and I could attend at the last minute.

We arrived at the Frankfurt airport and needed to take a train to the town where the ashram was. I remember being so impressed with the modern technology that we saw there. There was a small escalator next to the standing escalator, just for luggage to ride on, and in another part of the airport, the carts on which we pushed our luggage, flattened out their wheels when it was time to step onto the escalator and rode up with you. There was nothing like this in America and it very much made me think of how well Mercedes Benz were made and that these same minds which had invented them had created these high end extras at the airport.

When we finally arrived at the ashram, I was surprised by how old and large the building was. It was like something out of an old movie, a former manor turned into a spiritual center. We went into the large foyer and then into the dining room where people were having lunch. We saw a few familiar faces from the states and I was glad, but I didn't see any teenagers there as I was hoping would be for my daughter's sake. She knew a number of the teens and kids from the children's program, but none were to be found. Anyway, she was happy when the adults who knew her began to talk to her and I could see she was at ease.

I was told that the guru had not yet arrived and so after snacking, we went to our rooms. The rooms were bleak, just two bunk beds in a dorm-like room, but we didn't know what to expect. I left her to unpack and rest and went back downstairs. By the time I got down there, I was told that he had in fact arrived, and I walked out of the hall to a private corner and immediately broke down into tears. Just the idea that he was there near me, made me fill with emotion. I had missed him so so much. And then in my head he said, "You cry when I'm here, you cry when I'm not here?" joking at me in a loving way. That was always how he was inside, so personal and funny, he knew exactly just what little thing to say to make me laugh, internally he had become my very best friend.

Not long after this internal exchange, he floated down the stairs with a few devotees behind him. He smiled, acknowledging me and I joined the group and walked into the dining room with him. He greeted everyone who was present and stayed for about fifteen minutes, and then the small group of us who were "with him" followed him up the stairs and into his chambers. It was sooo nice to be easily allowed in (most of the time it was more difficult and painful than I can describe.) Perhaps because I didn't push like some of the others, or perhaps because I was too afraid to try; but because of the special way that he had treated me in Montreal, I just followed and entered.

When we got in, the brother of one of his top teachers whom I had seen at a Satsang in Montreal was obviously completely in love with the guru, opened up a space for me to sit near him, telling the other men present that I could be there. He obviously had some pull with the others and obviously was unaware of my feelings or the ways in which he and I had been relating. I accepted his generosity and sat up close. During our little visit with him, an ashram staff member came in and handed him a cell phone telling him that he had a call from India. I could almost make out the sound of a woman on the other end, seemingly scolding him, for things that were going on there. He did not seem annoyed but smiling at this "scolding". I got the impression that he liked the idea of a woman calling him and bugging him about things. I sat there wondering, why I didn't have his cell phone number, and yes I had called a few times to the ashram line, and had spoken with him once or twice, but it was quite difficult to get through.

We stayed for only a short time when someone came in and said that it was time to go down for a short afternoon Satsang. We all left with him and the six or so of us stayed close with him throughout. When it was over, we followed him back up, the crowd had gotten a bit larger and so he slightly ran up the steps, when we got to a certain turn in the stairs, his male head teacher, the mean one who had interrupted us in Santa Barbara, shoved his hand palm up two inches in front of my face saying, "STOP", with or without words, I don't remember. I simply remember the brunt force of his cruelty. This abruptness, in such a time of joy, of having been allowed to be with him for some time, again stunned me. The great love and joy that I had been feeling was quickly replaced by pain and hatred. I hated that teacher for his brusqueness and I also hated the guru for him allowing me to be treated thus. I walked myself down into the basement into a quiet place and proceeded to scream and cry out my hate.

After that, my hate could not go away. All of the pain that I had felt over the years, all of the hurt that had been inflicted upon me by the organization and by the lack of response from the man filled me to the brim and I could not shake it off. I spent my time with my daughter and going about the planned activities, but I wanted NOTHING more to do with him. A day or so later, while walking through one of the narrow corridors in the ashram, the guru appeared directly in front of me with a train of female devotees following behind him looking as if they were going to his chambers. He looked up and saw me and said, "COME," the words in the past, I had always wanted to hear from him, but I retorted with a very hard "NO!" The women looked shocked to hear me repudiate him. I could have cared less; so filled with venom and distaste. In fact, I was so fed up, that I refused to any longer be the beautiful woman that I had re-created myself into for him. At Satsang that night, I came in sweatpants and a jacket. Normally, I had on the most beautiful clothes, which I had bought at an expensive Pakistani store in Los Angeles. The owner of the store also made dresses for Barbara Streisand. I made myself THE most gorgeous for him. That was over. I went in my plain clothes, hair imperfect and face revealing the truth of the life I had been leading internally for so long. Hurt, sad and face swollen from all of the tears that I had shed and covered by absolute anger, I no longer chose to hide the truth of my existence with a shined up smiling face. I happened to notice that two of his head teachers, the beautiful man and the Indian woman, were both trying to get me to smile, to lighten me up, as the change in me was sooo very apparent. But I was unmoved. I saw them look up at him, as if to get him to do something to get the scowl off of my face. But his reply was, "Not to worry, I can handle people's anger." This Christmas trip turned out to be the most painful experience of our entire time together.

However, as things always did, he somehow began to work it out so that my anger began to lessen. Perhaps it was during a powerful healing session that I gave while there. I was again offering my energy healing abilities while at the course for donations to the ashram. This was an international course and there was a large group present from Japan. I had become friends with the group, through a number of healing sessions that individuals had scheduled with me. They had booked a tour bus to go on an outing to a nearby city, and because I wanted both to get away from the guru and to allow my daughter to see a bit more of Germany, we joined this group for the day. We had a lovely visit, actually to Strasbourg, France, which was not far away and eventually returned to the ashram. That night, one of the men from the group who I had met who was suffering from terminal cancer, had booked a late night session with me, after Satsang.

It began like all of my other treatments, patient laying on the table, me standing a few inches from his head and tuning into him. Then I scanned his body with my hands, and my hands were always drawn like magnets to the place in need of healing. My work was usually twelve inches or so from the body and I moved, to each place that was unwell. After about 40 minutes or so working on him, I began to feel myself going into a much deeper state of meditation almost trance-like, not like my normal work; he was of course in a very deep state as well. After awhile, my body was taken back away from him on the table and the energy force sat it into the chair, which was about two and a half feet from the table and the man. As I sat, the energy continued to pour and pour into my crown chakra, almost to the point of burning. And then, in the deepest state of Samadhi, I felt the crown of my head - my actual bones in my skull - begin to open up. It was as if someone or something were pulling my skull apart from the top center, my understanding of it now, is that my sutures were being vibrationally opened up, at the time, however, it was a happening that was unexplainable and unimaginable, and however I was not in a "thinking" place. There was no pain involved, and so I simply under the weight of this influence, allowed what was happening to happen. My body was lying back on the chair almost prone, head back as this opening continued to occur; until there came a point, where an energy poured up and out of the opening from my own head and hovered above my head, maybe four feet high in the air above my body. It felt as if it were in the shape of a triangle, with the bottom angle coming from the center of my head and the two wider angles about three feet out to each side of me in the air. However, when it was at its highest point, it somewhat curved over me in front of my body about six to ten inches. As I sat there, with this energy field over and around me, the man's body on the table began to flap up and down like a fish out of water, non-stop.

This powerful experience continued for over a half an hour. There was no thinking; there was only being. My being completely exposed to the universe, my shakti completely unleashed. I had no way to mentally comprehend what was going on, or of its importance, I was only an observer of the power of Life. At some point, the man's body began to settle and I began to come back into mine. When I finally saw him begin to stir, and I knew he was okay, I slowly got up from my seat, went to him and whispered in his ear to lie for as long as he desired, walked my way out of the room in the direction of the guru's quarters, laid my head down on the floor in front of his door and marveled at the powers of the universe unleashed through him and I.

This opening of my cranial sutures occurred on two other occurrences as well. Years later, I shared it with a world famous India Scholar who had written about this happening with his teacher. This man and I became friends, and he shared with me in person that I should not allow this to occur very often, as with other teachers they had died from it.

After that, things changed. He began to draw me to him in many ways. One afternoon while walking with him and a group, we got separated and so I simply made my way down to the meditation hall, knowing that eventually he would end up there. I stood at a window, watching him across the courtyard, standing inside the kitchen. I observed him with his group and his interactions. Finally realizing that he didn't seem to be on his way, I asked him internally if he wanted me to come to him, and he replied, "I will stay in this spot forever if you don't get here." And so I left and walked through the halls to join him. As I walked up to him with the group, and stood close, I felt something occur between our two hips. It not only felt, but also sounded like a bolt locking into place. A "humph" that was energetic and yet I also heard it. We then moved from that spot which he had been glued to for at least 15 minutes, and the two of us toured the rest of the kitchen, checking on the dinner and talking to the cook. I noticed her look at me with a smile and an air of respect and awe as if she understood what was going on between us.

Even though it wasn't one of the things that I was most attracted to in him, the guru with all of his wisdom and power was also like a big kid. He loved doing fun things like watching I Love Lucy on TV, squirting the crowds with huge water guns and generally playing. One day in Germany about twenty-five of us went out for a walk with the guru in the snow. I remember some of the guys wanted to take him for a little sledding or some fun in the snow, I remember as we walked, he looked at me as if a little embarrassed that I would see him behaving like such a kid. As internal as he was, there was also a part of him that wanted to "look" good.

I had also become friendly with the woman in the room next to mine. She was the new teacher put in charge of the Montreal Ashram. One day, she happened to share with me how happy she was to beat the course. She said that she didn't have the money; but that the guru had insisted upon her coming and that he paid for her ticket. He also was paying for her to go to the Italy New Year's Eve course. I was stunned, as I did not have enough money to get to Italy and I didn't know that he would actually pay someone's way. I felt that perhaps this information was coming to me for a reason, and so, later that day while walking with him, I asked him if he could help me to get to the Italy course. He responded that he was the "spiritual leader" of the organization and did not handle the financial matters. I was very disappointed.

Another afternoon, I found myself sitting in the foyer of the building, next to the fireplace. An older Indian couple was sitting nearby. We started a conversation, sharing where we lived and how long we had been involved in the organization. We talked about our children and I shared that mine was with me on the course, but was upstairs in the room. They spoke about their children both male and female who were grown and living in India. I casually asked if their kids were connected with the group. And to my surprise, the wife, turned and looked at me with an attitude of disbelief and replied, "Of course! My children do what I do!" Her self-righteousness and insistence, really took hold of me. "My children do what I do!" I realized was not the view that I, or most Americans, had. It sunk into me on many levels. Realizing that I had forgotten or never even considered that the Divine had made *me* the Mom and that therefore, I would *know* what is best for my child. Very unlike the American way of raising kids in which we give them so many options and pretty much let them run their lives. It was a very empowering moment for me as a Mother. As a result of this I realized that I should have *taken* her with me to India on that first trip. And of course, a different outcome would have occurred, but it also would have been perfect. From then on, even though she was almost 17 at that point, I had a different point of view in Mothering. Inside I was as solid as steel and although too late to force her to do anything, I was absolute in my *knowingness* of what she required. And beautifully, she fell directly into alignment.

For some reason, I decided to stay in the comfy chair by the fireplace after the couple had left. I sat there alone, simply enjoying the fire and especially the peacefulness of the late afternoon sky. A few moments later, a young Indian man walked down the large staircase dressed in a beautiful white coat. When he walked up to me, I commented on how attractive his coat was. He said, "the guru let me wear it, we are about to go for a ride with him to see the Christmas lights in town." I was surprised at the guru's generosity with his own personal items, but knew how kind he could be. I also thought that there was no coincidence that I had decided to stay seated here all by myself and receive this information about the ride into the city. So, with the assistance of the energy within as well as my own knowingness, I decided to climb the staircase and go to my room to get a coat, so that I too could be ready to go for the ride to see the lights.

There was no rush, my body took its time and got the coat and came back to my seat in the foyer, which was still empty. I sat and waited. After only a few minutes upon my return, he descended the staircase, wrapped in a beautiful white wool shawl. There were about fifteen devotees following him. He came down the landing and immediately walked up to me. It was raining outside and I had also grabbed an umbrella. We walked arm in arm under the umbrella out the door together. He greeted me and we spoke sweetly as we walked. I said to him, "I heard that you were going into the city to see the Christmas lights. Can I come?" He replied in the sweetest voice, "The car is full..." with a higher pitch at the end almost like a song. My heart sank as we walked silently the rest of the way to the awaiting van. The group of us stood circling the van, with both passenger sliding doors open. He and I stood next to each other as he, one by one, called out a different name to enter the vehicle. He took his time, the whole process taking over twenty minutes. Finally there were only three seats left, his seat in the front next to the driver, and the two passenger seats directly in front of me. He then did something that I had never seen him do, he called the next man's name and as he was about to enter on the remaining middle seats, the guru told him, "No, you sit in the front." The man was stunned as was everyone else, as the guru *always* sat in the front passenger seat. The man turned and looked at him, and he again told him, 'sit in the front." And so he did, leaving the two middle row seats directly in front of me open. I was trembling, praying that he would say my name, aware that I could have just stepped into the seat, but given that he was picking each passenger one by one, personally *and* that he had already told me that the car was full when I asked him if I could go along, I didn't dare. We all then stood for another three to five minutes before he finally called out another person's name, they jumped into the middle seat, and finally the guru then stepped into the remaining window seat. One of the men standing outside then, closed the door, and off they drove. I stood there in the freezing cold, stunned in disbelief and crushed.

After they left, the shock of what had just happened began to pour into my being. My body could not go back into the building; it just began to walk. Walk in the snow, walk in the unbelievable cold, just walk. As I began to climb up into the mountains, the hurt became completely and absolutely unbearable. I began to cry and scream uncontrollably. The anguish was on the physical, mental and emotional levels. I cried and cried the hardest this being, this body had ever cried. The hurt was just too much. After almost an hour I realized it was getting dark and I had better find my way back before I was completely lost, and so I drug my body through the icy snow back into the building. I knew I could not go to my room where my daughter might be, I could not allow her to see me in this place, and so I found a large empty room that we had held small group meetings in, and I went there and continued my purging. There almost were no words to what I was feeling. It was simply utter and complete devastation. I sobbed and sobbed until I couldn't move. And finally, I just lay there – empty.

After some time, I dragged myself back downstairs and sat my body back into that same seat in the entry. Simply being, waiting, I'm not sure, but eventually the door opened and he came in. He looked at me, I looked at him and you could see the damage that had been done to both of us. I asked him, how were the lights. He kind of grumbled that there were no lights, but it was obvious that he and everyone in the group were in a down dark mood and that could only be as a result of a change in him. I walked with him up the stairs, and it was apparent that he too was completely worn out. He could barely drag himself up the stairs, as could I. By then it was quite late, after eleven at night. I could feel the heavy energy within him; he could barely smile. And he did not speak. A few of us walked him to his door, but when we got to the top of the landing everyone left, there was only he and I. Silently, he stepped inside his door, however leaving it cracked open. Yet still, I had not the nerve or comprehension to go in.

The next morning after re-thinking all that had occurred, I realized, that he had in fact left the door open for me, and that even though he had said the car was full, he probably had wanted me to step inside, just take my place as he had left it next to him. I tried to understand why I couldn't see that before, but had no way of understanding my skewed perceptions. It had always been hard understanding men, but especially him. Most American men were so much clearer in their communication, and when he had said the car was full, I took him at his words. But now I could see that by the depth of his pain, he had in fact wanted me with him. I resolved to make up for my lack of knowing by getting up early and going to his room and be with him. I got dressed, went to his quarters and found about twenty or thirty people huddled on the floor outside of his door. I stepped over and thru them and knocked on his door. I was quite surprised when that same older Indian couple that I had been talking to in the foyer the day before, answered his door. I told them I wanted to see him, and they told me that he was not receiving any more visitors. I said please tell him that it is me, and they curtly, and in almost a protective manner said, "No."

I was hurt, I was finally ready to show up, to be with him and he refused me. I sat with the others for hours. Eventually, his head teacher, the younger Indian woman came out of his room, stepped over all of us, saw me and yelled out, "You Girl!" I was hurt that she would speak to me like that calling me a girl, much later realizing the reality of her words. My actions with him were much more like a teenage girl than a mature woman who knew what a man wants and needs.

Chapter Nineteen
The Kitchen Isn't Clean

It was the last night of the course and over three hundred of the course participants had boarded buses to head towards the big New Year's Eve celebration in Italy. Since he had not agreed to help me, as I did not have enough money to pay the full tuition for the course, I and my daughter were staying overnight and leaving for the airport in Frankfurt the next morning for her scheduled flight. There were about thirty people remaining at the ashram, including the guru, most of whom were ashram staff and those traveling directly with him. They were all leaving the next day to either drive or take a flight to Italy out of a different airport than we were. I remember walking past the office at some point that night before Satsang and overhearing some of the staff grumbling about the fact that he was changing his plans at the last minute and what a hassle it was for them…blah blah blah.., but I didn't pay it much attention.

I dressed and went down to the last Satsang, which was being held in a small hall, as there were so few of us remaining. I sat down around two rows back from the front and went into meditation awaiting his arrival. Submerged deep in Samadhi, suddenly and abruptly I was pulled out by a tapping on my shoulder. I opened my eyes and saw that it was one of the female staff, gesturing to me to come out to speak to her. I easily got up and followed her out of the hall up the stairs to a small room. Immediately another staff member came in and the two of them began to interrogate me. They wanted to know when I was planning on leaving the ashram, how I was going to the airport, why I was staying overnight, etc, etc. in a demanding tone. I was quite disturbed as they had pulled me out of Satsang and out of Samadhi for this? I angrily told them that my daughter and I were catching a flight early in the morning, that I was calling a taxi to pick us up to take us to the train station, that I didn't have the money to go to Italy and that was why I was still there. I was so upset by their grilling and probing, I wrongly assumed that *he* had sent them to do this. And for me, that was enough! The entire experience had been more pain than I could imagine, and I could no longer hold it in. And so I told them EVERYTHING. I told them of the years of him coming on to me. Of the sexual energy, of the mind control, of the airline ticket, of him canceling the talk in Montreal and staying with me, of everything that could make them understand that it was not me, or at least not all me. He was manipulating this situation and always had been; he never stopped; and I could not take it anymore. I cried and cried and cried, as I finally shared every intimate detail of my last few years.

Late that evening, I was sitting in the foyer, with a few people, one of whom was a teacher I had confided in. The guru walked down the stairs and went into the kitchen. Soon, he came out walking in a straight line to me, no one else, saying, "The kitchen isn't clean, they left the kitchen a mess." As he continued to walk towards me, I smiled at him and said, "not to worry, I will clean it". At the same time, that he spoke the words and physically came directly towards me, I heard that teacher say to someone sitting next to her, "See, there he goes again!" Meaning, he still is coming after me. I left the group, went into the kitchen and cleaned, as a woman would do.

Chapter Twenty
Can He Really Marry?

The next morning my daughter and I got up early to begin our journey home. When we were packed and ready to go, I left her to go and say good-bye to him. Walking to his door, it was early about 8:00am and very quiet in and around his door. I tapped gently, as to not wake him, if he were still asleep. Immediately he opened the door, and dressed in shorts and a t-shirt, said, "Hello, I am taking my bath," in a sweet sweet voice. I replied, "I just wanted to say good-by and tell you that I love you," and he replied, "I love you." I smiled, turned and walked away, as he closed the door.

My daughter and I then began out two-hour journey by taxi and train to the Frankfurt Airport. When we finally arrived, we got into the extremely long line to check-in her bags and once that was completed we would get in the shorter one and purchase my ticket. We had been standing in the approximately 50-passenger line, when my head lifted to a sight that was almost inconceivable. There walking through the airport, coming directly towards me at a fast pace was the guru and a small entourage of Indian men. I was shocked, and as the men saw me, they too were obviously taken aback; as I could see the disbelief on their faces of almost, "Oh no, my god he really *is* with her." And my daughter, who never really believed that he was for me, actually turned to me and asked the question: "Can he *really* marry?" The guru on the other hand, was as calm and collected as always, Mr. Cool. He walked right up to me, smiled and as I turned to my daughter, telling her I would leave her in her baggage check line and would call her on her cell, I turned and joined him and the men with my bags in cart.

As I joined him, I began to tell him that I had made enough money from my healing sessions to pay for my flight to Italy and that I could join him. He immediately put his finger to his lips indicating for me to hush. At that moment I remembered one of his teachers in my first few months had told me that you should never ask the guru anything that he would have to answer "No" to. And so, I just turned off my desire and accepted my fate. We walked quickly in the direction of his flight, as it was taking off soon. I then realized that what I had overheard in the office the night before was him changing his ticket from the airport on the other side of town where *everyone* else was flying out of to this airport where only *I* was flying from. And that was the cause of the angst that I had overheard by his staff. We continued over to the ticket counter for his flight. When we arrived, he was standing near the counter with his back to me about four feet away. From that position, we began to communicate psychically, like we always did when I was in Los Angeles and he was in some other part of the world.

We were standing there having this internal conversation while I'm looking at the back of his head, just as if we were miles apart and when suddenly he turned around and looked at me mid-sentence, with the biggest most beautiful smile I had ever seen in the years that I had known him or seen photos of him, flash at me. All of the men saw it as well. At that moment, the reservationist asked where they were flying to and he stepped up to the counter. She then must have asked for payment as he turned and asked for his black bag, which was on one of the carts with his luggage.

At that moment the other men with him went into a tizzy, as they were hurt by the idea that he would pay and they were insisting that they pay. He said, "No", and took his bag. He reached in and I saw something I had never seen before, the guru, with thousands of dollars in his hands. Again, I thought the men would faint, as if he was too holy to *touch* money. He then took out enough money to buy the tickets for all as I stood by silently, remembering that he had "shished" me and what the woman had said about *asking* him as well as remembering that I had already *asked* him at the ashram and he had replied about being the "spiritual leader"... Within a few moments, the transactions were made, the reservationist told them that they must hurry to catch the plane. I walked them a few feet forward to the entry of their gate, he turned back and said goodbye and he was gone.

I stood absolutely still in disbelief of both his coming and going, without me. And immediately, I was filled with the most powerful, highest vibration of energy. I tingled from the top of my head to the soles of my feet. I became at once, absolutely vibrational. So much so that I knew, that if I thought a thought it would manifest in front of me. I returned to my child, joined her and flew home to America. However, this powerful vibration stayed in me and thru me over the next few days.

When I was in my late 30's I had a dream that I would meet my husband when I was 42, in fact he came to my door dressed in a trench coat and a hat (in disguise) so that I could not see his face or clothes. In the second half of that dream, I was going to a New Year's Eve dance with my husband, but as we were about to begin dancing, I looked around and saw all of my girlfriends without a man, and I let him go and be with them instead.

Chapter Twenty-One
The Fire

After the excruciating pain and disappointment in Germany I made a decision to return to Los Angeles and focus my attention back on my daughter, who was completing her last year of high school. I continued to work at the pediatric pain program at the hospital, had begun teaching yoga at a studio near the beach, and continued to do temporary work to fill in the financial gaps. While on one temporary assignment, filling in for a woman on vacation, I looked up at the cloth divider of her cubicle and saw a quotation that she had pinned on it. I was stunned as I read the words; it was a beautiful spiritual quote in which the person writing was describing his love for God. What shocked me was that he was describing this love as if he was in love with God as his lover; the actual way that I felt. I had never heard anyone who loved the Divine as I did, with my whole heart, my whole soul, my whole body. My entire being was enraptured with Spirit. After reading the quote I immediately got on line to read about this man, Guru Nanak, to find out more about him. A few days later, or perhaps even that same day, I went out and bought a book about his life.

Not long after this, my good friend, the public health professor at UCLA who had assisted me with the ticket to Montreal, informed me that she had written a grant to bring nutrition and health into her church community, which was in the Black Community. She had included a yoga course as part of the grant. When she became aware that I was teaching yoga, she asked if I would like to teach both the Senior Yoga class as well as the beginning yoga class, which the grant was paying for. I, of course, agreed. I had been teaching yoga with the breath course for some time, and felt quite comfortable with that; but for senior yoga, I realized that I needed to do some research. I went to the library to look for books focusing on both chair and gentle yoga. While searching, I came across a book entitled <u>Yoga for Health and Healing</u>. It was a wonderful book in which it described yoga postures for almost every ailment imaginable in and A-Z format. I checked it out for as long as possible as well as the books for the seniors, and realized that I needed to own it. I telephoned the publisher of the book as she was located nearby in the Los Angeles area; and she informed me that she was no longer publishing it, but had several copies at her home and invited me to stop by and purchase one. I was delighted. When we met I told her how much I enjoyed the postures I had already tried and that they had brought great relief to whatever issue I was trying to improve. She told me that if I was interested in taking classes in this type of yoga that there was a group which she use to be a part of, but no longer was, that taught that style of yoga regularly right in the West Los Angeles area, where I lived and that it was called "Kundalini Yoga".

I decided to attend a class and found them quite enjoyable and yet quite different than the gentle Hatha type yoga postures that we had practiced and taught in our group. What I appreciated most was that the practices focused on specific issues, such as the chakras, or the mind, or the heart, etc.; and although I was and am still not a very physically active person, much more calm and meditative in my practices, I very much loved as well as benefited from the rigorousness of the yoga. They were not difficult postures, but intensely energizing ones. I felt a new level of vitality that I had not experienced in my life, except perhaps in my youth during sports and dance.

Both this "Kundalini Yoga" (which I found the title interesting because I knew that the "Kundalini" was not something that could be captured by a teaching or a brand, like the air it simply was) and the Art of Living program included powerful breathing practices. However, I found them completely different, yet helpful in unique ways. I of course had gone through my spiritual transformation (had my *actual*

Kundalini Shakti rising) through my relationship with my guru and thru the Art of Living Healing Breath Course and practices, and yet, I remember at one point returning to him after a period of time and he saw me and said, "Kamala, you are so bright!" This I knew was a direct result of these powerful Kundalini Yoga practices. Both were special and yet still I felt more at home with the more Satvic (peaceful) and Bhakti (loving) nature of the guru's work as opposed to what I felt was a stronger, yet harsh (sword-like) energy of the other.

While working with the children at the hospital, I began to feel and know that it would be helpful to teach them yoga in order to assist them in another way in their healing process; so that they would have ongoing healing tools for their life. As an energy healer at the hospital there were no "certifications" to do what I did. To make it "sound" more official, my badge said "Dr. Easton", even though my Ph.D. was in education, and that I was a "Bio-energy Therapist", whatever that might be. However, I knew that if I wanted to teach yoga I would need to be certified for the hospital to approve. And so, I decided to get my yoga certification and do it in Kundalini Yoga, as I was very much enjoying the classes and it was very close to the house that I was renting. (I had been offered to rent the back half of a house of a woman who was in our spiritual group where there were two bedrooms and two baths for my daughter and myself.)

The teacher training program was a six month certification process where we met every other weekend. I very much enjoyed learning the exercises and the technology behind the program. However, I did feel somewhat uncomfortable with the Sikh mantras, as the Sanskrit mantras, which our spiritual group chanted struck a deep chord within. Even though initially I was adverse to them, that had changed but felt that a language, which was from a religion that was created so recently (the Sikh Religion is only 500- or so years-old) might not have the same power as an ancient one. And still, I willingly participated and followed the program including the cold morning showers for the entire six months. About three months into the program, I was sitting on the floor in class towards the back of the large yoga room; my head turned and looked up at a group of paintings hanging on the wall and my eyes began to focus in on one in particular. I sat starring at it and realized that it was a remarkable resemblance to Guru Nanak, whose book I owned and whose heart

I had connected with. I paused and then raised my hand to ask my teacher who was on the stage, in a puzzled voice, "Guru X., Is that Guru Nanak?" And he responded, "Yes, Kamala, he *founded* the Sikhs." My eyes opened wide with surprise and I was taken aback. First, that I had never noticed the paintings, which obviously had been hanging there the entire three months of the training and even the months before when I was taking classes. But more importantly because, in my love of reading the words of this beautiful man, I had completely skipped over or at least did not remember reading what he had actually *done* on the earthly level; as I was so enraptured by his deep love of God. I could not believe that this being who I felt so connected with, had either shown up in my life, yet again, or had drawn me into his dharma. I could do nothing but smile. And of course, it lessened my resistance to his mantras.

One afternoon, a few months after I had completed my teacher training, I had just ended a beautiful Kundalini Yoga class, in the late afternoon. I offered a classmate, who was also an energy-healing client of mine, a ride home, but needed to go by my house on the way. We rode slowly, enjoying the beautiful Southern California day. As I turned onto my street, I hesitated as I noticed that there were a number of vehicles in the middle of the street. As I drove further down the block, I grew concerned as I saw fire engines. Immediately, we stopped our conversation to take in whatever was going on, and slowly as we drove and got closer I realized that the fire engines were directly in front of the house in which I lived. I looked and watched as the firemen came out of the house and realized that there had actually been a fire there. My heart began to beat rapidly and both my friend and I began to panic as I told her that it was the house that I rented. Stunned, we got out of the car and went up to the firemen who told me there had been a fire in the back of the house, the back, in fact was where my rooms were. The owner was not home, but out came the painter who had, over the past few weeks, been repainting almost every room in the house. Eventually they let me walk in, and I found my entire room, completely burnt, everything in it including the roof black and ashed. I asked both the painter and the fireman what had happened, but no one seemed to know. They guessed that it might have been some combination of electrical wiring or perhaps the paint. I simply froze. Froze with fear that my friend did not yet know, froze with disbelief that everything that I owned was gone. Thankfully, the rest of the house, other than smelling like smoke, was not very damaged including my daughter's room, which although on the back of the house with mine, was on the opposite side. Immediately I telephoned the owner and informed her of the devastation. She couldn't believe it and immediately came home.

For a few nights my daughter and I were put up in a motel by the Red Cross, the owner's insurance put her and her partner up in a 5-star hotel...... After that, we lived separately again, as she went to stay with a friend's family from her school, so that she could get in every day, and I stayed with a friend of mine from the group. A few days later, I returned to the house to try to salvage anything of mine that could be found, but there was NOTHING. I went to what had been my book case, where my art that I had purchased in my earlier days while living in Manhattan once hung or stood, but there was nothing to be seen. I looked down on the ground, in the midst of all of the soot and noticed something green. I picked it up and there was the Guru Nanak book, blackened on one corner, yet still legible. I couldn't believe it.

I walked to a pile of burnt rubble and melted plastic and realized that that was where my closet had been and that there had been a plastic three-drawer container where I kept some of my clothes. On top of it had been all of my sarees, which were gone, but hidden underneath I kept a very special copy of the Bhagavad Gita, that the teacher who's organization I had learned my energy healing from had translated. It was very powerful, but inside that book is where I had hidden the very personal pictures I had taken of the guru stepping wet out of the Ganges in Rishikesh. And when I brushed aside the ashes, there, *completely* untinged, was the book, a bright blue paperback, and inside every picture of him, in PERFECT condition... And as all of his "spiritual" pictures had burnt, I knew, at that moment, that he was calling me back to him, as a man, not as guru.

I learned from this experience that Renunciation is a happening, not something that we do. If required, the Divine will take away our earthly attachments. Those who say they are going to" become" a renunciate, may in fact have nothing but their ego becoming.

e-mail
Ravi,

There truly are no words to describe my life. The loss of everything over the past two years, culminating in the fire, has left me standing on my toes, with nothing solid to stand on in this earth, ready to simply fly. I have at the same time become stronger inside, handling each of my fears and tendencies that are self-defeating. My daughter is again living one place, and I another. God knows the answer is not to rebuild a temporary setting yet again. There is nothing left in my life except the deep love, bliss and unbelievable experiences that I have had from knowing you. I can't believe there is any place on earth that I am supposed to be, but with you. I no longer can stand the pain of a life away from my love. Please pull me to you.

Chapter Twenty-Two
Confrontation at the Indian Ashram

Not long after the fire I returned to India, realizing that my attempts to lead a normal life and get my daughter through her senior year were futile, after trying and having everything burned to the ground. While there, she continued to stay with the friends who took her in after the fire. The time right before the fire I had met a very interesting Indian businessman. He and a group of colleagues were touring the world in the attempt to gather research and information as to what makes the best form of education. It was fascinating to hear that these businessmen, began with the question "Should there be education in a society?" and then proceeded on to visit and learn from the most successful schools on the entire planet including UCLA's elementary school where my daughter had attended. One of my colleagues in education told me about him and a meeting was arranged. He was looking for teachers, not necessarily with a background in teaching, but people who could bring their particular areas of expertise into the classroom. I was very intrigued by the idea and felt that perhaps a job in India would be a good solution for my state of disarray and my desire to be in India.

I e-mailed the guru telling him of the fire and that I had received some insurance money and that I was coming to India to meet with this man in Ahmendabad (a northern city in the state of Gujarat). I also said that I needed to be with him, given all that had occurred. I received an e-mail back from the ashram informing me that the guru would be traveling during my stay and therefore there was no reason to come to the ashram. But with the prospects of a job and the absolute devastation of my life, I went ahead. When I arrived at the airport, even though it was a different state far away from Bangalore, it was the same smell, the same heat, the same feel; it was all India. I didn't realize how much I had missed it and how much it was home

Mr. S. had me met at the airport by a driver and arranged for me to stay at an apartment in the city, which he owned. The school was out in the countryside and the plan was to go to it by the next day or so. The following morning he picked me up and arranged for a few days for me to experience that part of India. He gave me a personal tour of his company, from which he used the funds to create the educational foundation. I enjoyed meeting his staff, who were extremely friendly and informative. He also took me around the city, which included the university that he had attended, a quite impressive business institute with exceptional modern architecture. He took me shopping, where I purchased the most exquisite sheer silk organza tye-dye saree that I had ever seen, a temple tour and finally he offered me my choice of the best restaurants in Ahmedabad; a modern 5-star one or a traditional village style set out in the country. I chose the traditional village themed one and we set off on our ride outside of the city. The restaurant was marvelous, with a long entryway of luminary candle bags on the path guiding us in. Once inside we needed to decide if we would go straightaway to eat or take a tour of their museum. I wanted to see the museum, which was a fascinating display of ancient utensils for cooking and eating. I was surprised when I saw that many utensils, which I thought were modern inventions, had already been around for thousands of years. We then went to another section of the restaurant and waited for our food, while watching a live fire-eating show in an open-air arena. Finally, we came to the main dining area, which was also open-aired but with a thatched roof. We sat on the floor at the lowered tables and were served the best food I had ever tasted. To this day it remains one of my favorite restaurants in the world.

The next day, I toured the school; meeting the teachers, students and seeing the grounds. I was impressed by how much he had done and was continuing to do by building a teachers' training institute right on the property and was amazed by the stories that I had learned about the challenges of offering scholarships to street children and having them attend classes with upper class kids, and the issues that their families had. Mr. S was a remarkable man, taking on challenge after challenge and helping many along the way. I very much enjoyed a friendship with Mr. S for many years, sharing with him some of my spiritual experiences and beliefs. During that next year, he shared with me spiritual shifts that he had after the time of our meeting.

Once in India of course, I decided to head on down to the ashram, whether he was there or not. I needed to at least try to see him. I realized long before that there was no trusting the e-mails from his people and that they screened everything. I needed to speak to the man about all that was happening in my life, especially what had occurred between us in Montreal. I sent an e-mail to someone who used to work closely with him, who I had met on my first visit and was now on the board at the ashram. I thought perhaps he could get a message to him. When I arrived at the ashram, I went immediately to his house. I did not want to have to deal with his people. When I arrived at the top of the long steps to his house, there he was standing out front with a group of people. I was so surprised to see him. Emotionless, he greeted me and said, "Kamala, you've come a long way." Tongue-tied, I replied, "there was no distance that could keep me from you." We walked together for a little while, but I could not seem to get out any words as he was with his group and I was caught off guard to run into him. He then told me to go and get into my room and unpack. One of his extremely handsome young white-robed men who I remembered from my first visit escorted me to my room, which was on the other side of the ashram that had been built up since my last visit. I was amazed at how much construction had gone on since my last visit. When we arrived at my room, this young man reminded me in an arrogant tone that, "this is a much nicer room than where you stayed when you were here before." Insinuating that I had stayed in a lower class room and therefore had not had much money. I just said, "Thank you", and went in to unpack.

I couldn't believe I was actually there. After almost two years. I rested from my journey; however still confused about the greeting and not quite feeling like myself, but also not feeling at home. There was a special celebration going on at the ashram and, as always, many people waiting to see him. A day went by without being able to see him and I simply began to become depressed and retreat. I did not go to the afternoon celebration, but stayed in and slept; but in the middle of my rest, there was a loud gunshot that went off, at the celebration, and it startled me out of my sleep and in my mind he yelled at me for not having attended. That night, there was a huge Satsang with more than 5000 present and I was far away from the stage and up on a hill. When Satsang began, a beautiful woman stepped onto the stage and slowly walked the long runway to him, with a white organza and gold train behind her, went to him with arti in hand and proceeded to kneel in front of him to perform it. He, then took the arti from her hands and lifted it around her in honor of her beauty and courage. I was taken aback; angered over his gesture, angered over her taking the stage with him, but more angered over my inability to do the same.

The next day he came to me internally and yelled, "If you don't like something, SAY SOMETHING!" In my mind I yelled back at him, "Well, I am NOT, coming over *there* again to try and see you! If you come to ME, then I will TELL YOU!" Within 15 minutes, I heard a commotion outside of my rooms and I went outside to ask someone what was going on. The woman next door replied that the guru was taking a walk just past my building with a few devotees and that they had just gone by. And so I realized he *had* come to me.

Quickly I got myself together and ran down the stairs to try to catch up with his group. When I reached him, he was with a reporter, giving a walking interview. But when I caught up to the group and got upfront with him, I just didn't care who was there. We walked a little ahead of everyone and I just began to let him have it..."I can't believe I came all this way and I can't get in to see you! This isn't okay! I don't believe if you want me that you would let this keep happening!"... and anything else that I could think of. And he just stayed next to me and listened. I could tell the others were startled by my accusations, but they just stepped away and let us be.

That evening after Satsang I *was* allowed in his home; it was much easier. There was a group of about thirty of us and we laughed and talked with him for least forty-five minutes. When he said it was time to leave everyone rose and began to walk out slowly. I was one of the last to leave as I felt he was closer to me now. But as I got to the door I realized that there was one woman, one of his teachers from the ashram who was showing everyone out of the door, including myself. I was confused and not knowing how to handle the situation, as I had never stayed in his house in India; and so I felt that this woman from the ashram was being allowed to show us all out the door. And so I let her put me out and she closed the door. I was finished, angered, frustrated I didn't know how to say "no, this is not okay" or "no, I'm not leaving" I simply allowed myself to be pushed out.

The next morning when I awoke, I realized once again I had had enough. I decided to go to his house and speak to him about what had happened in Montréal and about the fire, and that my life was in utter confusion. I walked across the ashram to the bottom of the steps and saw that there were no guards on duty, so I proceeded up the steps to his house. When I arrived at the beautiful wooden door and knocked I was allowed in again easily. He was in his seat talking to a small group of people, perhaps ten or so, and I joined them and sat down. Once again my needing immediate attention was pacified by the ease at which I was allowed in, a not very familiar occurrence for me, and to simply be sitting with him. We spoke to him for about fifteen minutes, when he then rose and said he was going to rest and stood up and walked out the rear door of the room. In that moment I realized how ignorant I had been as I actually thought that this small room was his house. Because we always left the room before him I had never seen the other door open and had never seen the additional quarters. That is when I realized that the woman the night before and other people have always gone into his *house* and that I was always in the waiting room or the meeting room. When he opened the door and went through into the other room, I got a glimpse of his *actual* house. I was hurt and angered beyond my comprehension, that all of this time I had been taking *nothing*.

As everyone stood up to leave the room, I simply re-fused. I re-fused. The room had cleared, with the exception of a few ashram staff; but I did not get up from my seat. One teacher then approached me and said, "Hello, it's time to go" I said nothing. Again he said, "Okay, it is now time for you to go!" with more insistence. I replied, "I am not going until I speak to him." I was in a state of absolute fearlessness; deeply centered in my knowingness, stronger than I had ever been. Immediately they sent one man out the door and within about five minutes one of his head teacher's who knew me came into the room. He walked over to me and said, "Kamala, you really need to go, it is time." I turned to him and said, "I am not going until I speak to the guru." He replied, "The guru has gone to rest you, must go." I said nothing and just stayed still. I was immobile; I was as solid rock. There was a firmness and righteousness in me that I had never felt in my life I absolutely knew that I needed to speak with him that I would not be deterred *and* that it was my right. That teacher standing above me continued, "Look at what are you doing, you have to go now." I then began to share with him, why I was staying, some of the personal things that had occurred with the guru and that I was not going anywhere until I spoke with him. He quickly left and went thru that back door into the guru's quarters, within a few minutes the guru entered, came over to me and stood above me with the other men and asked me what I was doing. I immediately broke down into tears and began to shout, "You know what you did! You showed me you wanted me! You told me you loved me! My house burned down and my life is in shambles!" I revealed details with all of them standing around me in a circle. I accused him to his face, and he denied nothing. They all simply stood around me in silence while I had had my say. I began to just cry and I got up and ran out the door.

I began to walk fast to my room on the other side of the ashram. I just wanted to go! Following me was the pretty faced "ashramite" who had helped me into my room just a few days before. I was walking extremely upset when the young man turned to me and yelled at me, "Get Out Now!" adding great insult to my already injured being. I turned around to him and yelled that I was on my way to pack up and go, and he so angered me in my time of upsetness, that I screamed at him that if he had experienced what I had experienced with the guru every day, he wouldn't be saying anything to me!

When I turned to him, he started to run away from me in fear like a scared kid as if I was going to hit him. I screamed at him to leave me alone and I immediately went to my room packed up everything that was there and left the ashram.

Realizing that I was not yet ready to leave India, but that I had had enough of him and of the ashram mistreatment, I decided to stay and take a yoga teacher training course since I was in India. As I had previously thought about this, in case the ashram did not let me come, I had contacted a yoga-training course right in Bangalore. I immediately telephoned the small yoga ashram on the outskirts of Bangalore and asked them when the next class was beginning. I was told that I could come immediately and that the classes would resume as I was there that they could bring me right into the current class that was being offered and that sleeping and eating accommodations were part of the weeklong teacher training course. I did not contact the guru or the ashram as to where I had gone; I simply wanted to be distanced from all of it. I immediately took a taxi to this ashram and found a very small, yet peaceful compound that had lovely green grass in the center of it (something I hadn't seen much of in India) and perhaps four or five bungalow buildings surrounding it.

I went into the office and met a beautiful older woman, who welcomed me and registered me into the program and gave me a tour. She showed me to my room, which was very barren and basic but good enough; clean and well kept; with a shower and everything I needed. She told me what time dinner was served and that I would meet the swami in charge of the classes at that time. I showered, and rested and felt healed and I came out for dinner and was pleased to meet a very tall dark-skinned distinguished Indian older gentleman who was the swami/yoga teacher. He welcomed me with grace and kindness and it felt so good to be received with love, as I had been on edge for so long not knowing who I could trust and whether or not I was safe at the Art of Living Ashram. Even though there was a full schedule of classes for the next seven days, I could rest in their hearts and I was thoroughly grateful.

The next day I needed to go out of the ashram to use an Internet Café which wasn't far away. As I walked out of the grounds I looked up and was greatly and pleasantly surprised to see a beautiful young Black American woman walking in. Even though I was sure she was American I still had to ask as I had never seen another Black American in India (first or second trip). She responded that yes, she was from California. We stood and chatted for awhile and then agreed to have lunch together as I was getting ready to run my errands and she was coming to check in for the class as well.

What a coincidence! I went into town where I was e-mailing my daughter and when I returned the young woman, J, and I met for our lunch. I was so anxious to hear what she was doing in Bangalore, or in India in general. She proceeded to tell me about the wonderful program that she was a part of. J was a graduate student participating in a traveling journalism program funded by the Sony Corporation. They had hired ten to twenty students to travel the world and conduct interviews on various subjects, videotape them, type them up, and then through the Internet, send them back to American middle- school classrooms. Each intern was given a laptop and a video camera in order to conduct their interviews and send them to the schools on a weekly basis. It was one of the most exciting programs I had ever heard of. She said that they were more than halfway through the year-long program and had traveled to more than twenty countries already. I was quite impressed. She was kind, energetic, beautiful, as well as intelligent. I was so proudly happy to meet this young black woman.

The next day, we decided to go shopping together in the city. As we met in the courtyard, I was quite surprised to see her, as she looked lovely in her dark red, black and green saree. In these African colors she looked like an African Indian Princess. And although she had very little money on her internship budget, and as it turned out I did have funds as a result of partial insurance monies from the fire. However when we entered the Indian shops, I in my pure cotton outfit, which was perhaps regarded by Indians as "poor people's clothing" (as Indians with money no longer wear cotton... only the poorer people do) and so the shopkeepers paid me no attention. But my friend J in her polyester saree received all of the attention and assistance. It was one of those many eye-opening experiences that I observed as to the differences of Indian and American cultures.

The classes were wonderful learning traditional Hatha Yoga from this older Yogi/Swami who was kind and yet commanding and in charge. Immersing myself in his program helped me not only in my body but also in attaining a peace of mind, much of which had been lost through my experiences at the Art of Living ashram. The woman who was assisting at the ashram and who had registered me was also very welcoming and kind. She invited me to her home some evenings for dinner and took me shopping, as I told her that I very much wanted to learn Indian cooking and needed to purchase the stainless steel pots, pressure cookers and spice holders. I, and almost every woman in the Art of Living, wanted to cook for the guru, but I also just wanted to learn to cook Indian food.

After the course, I had eventually cooled down in regards to the guru, I did contact the ashram and was told that the guru was headed to Singapore and then to Jakarta for his birthday celebration. And since I was in that part of the world, I decided to see how difficult it would be to go. I went by a travel agency and found that it was not very expensive, although I was nearing the end of my funds and was having trouble getting my daughter to deposit monies into my account; I decided to change my flights and go as well. And so I did. I arrived in Singapore and was amazed. Other than hearing about the no chewing gum law, I thought it was a fantastic city: so, beautiful, modern and multicultural. In the airport, I met a couple who explained to me the four major ethnic groups and languages present there: Chinese, Malaysian, Indian and English. I visited shops, purchasing a new saree, ate at restaurants of the various cultures and also went to a large Hindu Temple. However, even though I was enjoying the sights, I arrived at my hotel and felt alone, as I wanted to be with him and the group. I was very much looking forward to his talk that evening. I took my time preparing, dressing in my exquisite silk sheer saree from Gujarat, allowing Spirit to guide my movements. When I did arrive by taxi the Satsang had already begun. Slowly and elegantly, I stepped into the middle of the group of about 250 people who were already meditating with him on the stage; all eyes were closed including his. However, before I sat down, I saw him open his eyes to see me. As I sat down, full of my power and beauty as a woman, I decided that I had had enough of him connecting with me vibrationally and internally only. That he needed to be confronted with the actuality of my being and my body. He needed to stop all of these internally alluring vibrations and relate to me as the real woman that I am. I sat there, and spoke to him in my head, but told him that I was a real woman sitting there with a real body and that he needed to be with me. I let him know that I was present, in every way. After awhile, I again looked up at the stage to be sure that he was perceiving me. And, it was obvious that he very much was.

His talk began with an introduction by a young, famous and exquisitely beautiful Indian actress. She spoke about his accomplishments and looked as if she knew him personally and loved him very much. During the middle of Satsang, I got up to use the ladies' room and coming out I walked directly into his sister, who hadn't spoken to me in some time, but who could not hold back the impact of my look in the saree. She spoke as if taken aback, "Kamala, you look *so* beautiful?!" I simply looked at her.

Just before Satsang ended, the energy raised me up from my seat, as always, and took me back out into the foyer. I stood and waited for him. Immediately, I was joined by the beautiful actress and one or two other female devotees. She had that confident look on her face, inwardly awaiting him. And, immediately I began to feel my own confidence fading. As I looked at her as yet another person in the "in crowd", who obviously was *with him* as she had been selected to introduce him, and I again, on the outside, not having had the external validation to be *with him*, I began to feel that he would not choose me, that he would not take *me*; completely forgetting the power I had had over him inside the Satsang, and over these years. When he did come off the stage, he walked directly towards our group, and I saw him look at me, seeing the change in me, my lacking in self-assuredness. I saw the disappointment and at the same time wonder on his face, as if "What happened?" And then he turned and saw her, gazing at him with love and confidence of his wanting her, and I think he understood. Immediately, he turned and with his sister, walked down the hallway away from all of us and out the back door of the hotel. After a few moments, I came back to my senses and walked hurriedly down the hall after him. But by that time, he was already in the parking lot inside his car. He rolled down the window to see what I wanted, and I asked if I could come with him and he said to just come by the house tomorrow. And that was that.

The next morning I awoke, ready to go to see him at the house. Internally he spoke to me and told me to pack up all of my things, check out of the hotel and bring them with me to the house. I was very upset and felt that there was no way that I could do that. He, the voice within kept insisting that I bring everything with me. I again refused. I continued to get dressed. He seemed to acquiesce and said to simply pack up everything, check out and leave my bags at the front desk in storage. I agreed that I could do that. I headed downstairs to check out; as soon as I had finished and was about to give them my bags, the voice said to me in a controlling voice, "Now get your bags and get in a taxi and come!" Shocked and somewhat amused by the slyness of it, I succumbed.

I took a taxi to the house and when I arrived saw that it was packed with over one hundred devotees crammed into the living area and there was no place to sit or stand. I left my bags outside with all of the shoes on the porch. I walked into the kitchen and spoke to someone and was told that everyone was waiting for him to come back downstairs. At some point, he came downstairs and had a nice talk with the crowd. He then suggested that everyone have lunch and went back up. I decided to follow him up the stairs to the room where he was staying. He came out of the room to talk to me in the hallway. I asked him if I could come to Jakarta for his birthday celebration. He then very sweetly replied that since his Mother had passed, he didn't like to make a big fuss about his birthdays or things like that. And that I should just skip it and go home. He told me to go and eat and then come up later. Somewhat disappointed, but not so much as he was so dear in his words and he did want to see me later, I followed his words and went downstairs to join the others.

After I finished my lunch and went back to his door, I was allowed in with him and three or four Indian women. They were sitting chatting. I asked him again if I could go to Jakarta, and again, he said, no, it would not be best. He then began to grill me about the saree that I had on. He asked me if I had recently purchased it. I said yes, he then asked me how much it cost, I told him. He went on to press me saying it was too much money to spend and that I couldn't afford it. I was quite embarrassed for him to be speaking about my personal finances in front of these women.

It was true that for some reason I was having a difficult time receiving a deposit into my account from my daughter. It seemed to have been stopped at every turn and I was quite frustrated. In fact, I had wondered if *he* had something to do with it. But, I had no idea why he was pushing this issue. He asked me where I was staying and I told him in a local hotel, he told me I did not have the funds for this. I got so frustrated that I then stood up, walked out of the room, down the stairs and out the door, picked up my bags, walked down the middle of the road, crying. I simply had no way of understanding his methods, and he always just seemed to end up hurting me. Perhaps he was trying to find a way to bring me into the group and house in which he was staying and traveling; to show the owner that I had no funds and needed to be cared for. But at the time, my mind never saw it from that perspective.

Even though he had told me not to go to Jakarta, I was angry and so I decided to go anyway. I arrived at the airport the next day with ticket in hand, my plane leaving a few hours after his. I found him with a small group at the airport and told him that I was coming. Immediately he turned to me in front of the women, some of whom had been in the room with him when he had told me not to go, and said, "OK, you can come!" It felt as if he were giving me his permission, since I was going anyways, and I could see that the women seemed somewhat disturbed at my arrival.

I arrived in Jakarta and stayed at the 4-Star Hotel that most of the others were also staying at. It was one of the nicest hotels that I had stayed at during my travels. And thankfully, Jakarta was inexpensive enough that I could. I especially remember the morning breakfast buffet, with hundreds of dishes, breakfasts from all around the world. I particularly liked a dal for breakfast with jaggery a raw Indian sweetener and cream added so that it was similar to oatmeal, but you were getting the protein of the beans instead of just oats. Given all that had occurred with my body, I found it extremely necessary to increase my protein intake while on a vegetarian diet.

That night I got dressed to go to the birthday Satsang. Dressing in another beautiful saree I took a taxi to the venue. It was a beautiful 5-star hotel and I entered and took a seat towards the front. But after sitting for awhile as the room began to fill up, I noticed that a few men in the back were staring at me. A woman had gone over to them and pointed towards me. The two of them moved to the row that I was in and stood behind it. I began to feel extremely uncomfortable. The guru entered, and they stood guard over me throughout the entire Satsang. I felt terrible, really hurt and afraid of what they might actually do. And at the same time wondering what in the world had been said about me, and what did they think I would do. I sat there throughout the entire birthday celebration, almost on the verge of tears, and not enjoying one moment.

When it finally was over, the guru decided to give darshan. He stayed seated and allowed each person present to come up and greet him and then exit the hall. I did not move from my seat as the men were still standing just four rows behind me. When almost everyone had gone on stage, there were only eight or ten of us left in the venue, I stood up and neared the stage, but still stood back. He then sat there, and looked at me with the most dreamy and longing eyes urging me to come up and greet him with his eyes. But I did not move, as I was not sure what the men were going to do if I moved near him. He continued to stare at me so completely lovingly and wantingly until one of the women present, came over closer to me and told me, "Go on up, he obviously wants you."

As I began to move slowly towards him, the men started getting closer, but then stopped. I went to him and told him that they were there and had been watching me, but he assured me that it was nonsense. He got up from his seat and we walked off the stage together, and then one of his closest American teachers who often plans his schedules, who I had asked to tell me where his after-birthday party was to be held, came up to us and then the two of them walked quickly ahead of me out the lobby. I followed but when we got to the front, his car was waiting and they stepped in, and one of the men standing outside his car immediately came up to me and blocked me with a rifle in his arm. It scared me to death. I had never ever been treated anything like that before in my life and had never come that close to a weapon. I was petrified. His car immediately drove off and I just stood there and at first screamed at the man, "How dare you do that!" and at the same time, crying in absolute hurt and shame.

I made it back to my hotel, simply broken. I cried most of the night. I cried until I couldn't cry anymore; until utter exhaustion took me over. The next day I did not wake up until late. I knew that there was a gathering at the house where he was staying, but I didn't want to go. In my mind, he begged me to come. And so finally, I got myself together as best I could, face and eyes completely swollen, put a shawl over my head and went. I arrived at one of the grandest homes, well actually the grandest home I have ever entered. It was like a museum. The foyer was huge, with a large two-story balcony around it, inside the house. Marble everywhere. I went in and slowly walked over to get something to drink, when a woman came up to me. She was the lady of the house and she came to me and apologized for how her husband had treated me the night before. She said that the guru was extremely upset with him, and had made everyone aware of it that night. She was very kind and considerate of my feelings. She told me he was in another room greeting people and to go and see him. I walked in and there was a small stage, and people were waiting in line to go up to meet with him. I got in the back of the line, continuing to cover my swollen face with my scarf and waited my turn. I noticed a number of women pointing to me and whispering, but I could not care anymore.

When I got up to him, he asked me how I was and then asked

me when I was leaving. I said I wasn't sure and then he said, "I'm going, you go!" And that was that. I left the house, went back to my hotel, packed my bags and returned to the U.S., somewhat aware that he had stood up for me at least to some extent.

> *Draft e-mail*
> *Ravi,*
>
> *I am in Los Angeles, trying with all my might to release the tremendous pain of this past month. I know that you had originally said not to come, but when the fire happened and I lost everything, and you had come to me in a dream telling me that on that day everything would begin to happen, I just felt that there was no place else for me to be but with you, in order to initiate this new beginning.*
>
> *What I gained from this trip was the ability to say, and often loudly, "THIS IS UNACCEPTABLE" when I was treated less than the best or terribly. I wish I had learned this lesson earlier, perhaps at the ashram when you did things to me which were UNACCEPTABLE, but some lessons take time.*
>
> *I can't be with a man who can not treat me like the wonderful woman that I am. A woman who deserves to be WITH a man. Not someone hidden in the background. A woman who deserves to ride in the car with a man, to travel with a man, to be with a man. I pray, that God in me, fills me with the strength to know this and to be this always, regardless of **who** that man is. Regardless of whether he is someone powerful and famous, regardless of whether he is quick with his voice and shuts me up quickly, regardless of anything, I am not to be pushed aside. I deserve to be spoken to kindly, respected and loved – like the way "THAT MAN" Who use to speak to me did.*
>
> *If he still exists, I welcome him into my life. If he is gone, it is very difficult for me to see happiness in my world right now, but I know I AM GOD, so ALL things must be in their right place.*

Chapter Twenty-Three
Cultural Ineptitude

In July, two months after his birthday in Jakarta, there was another Gurupurnima course in Lake Tahoe. I had registered and decided to drive up. I was determined that this time that he would be mine and that I would act like I knew that. He had already told me he loved me. And so why shouldn't I? I had finally learned to cook Indian food and had brought my pressure cookers and Indian spice holders and gone to Little India in Los Angeles and purchased the dahls and the spices. And so I decided that I was going to cook for him.

I arrived in time for evening Satsang. As it was nearing its end, my body as always, got picked up and walked towards the exit. Usually I got walked to the correct exit and waited for him, but this time, it walked all the way to my car in the parking lot, and so I got in and drove it to the entrance of the hall, obviously waiting for him. Usually someone was assigned or had decided in the "In Circle", to do that, or sometimes it was whoever got there first, but I then just said, "Yes, he is mine, I can drive him to his house!" I had rented a large, new, beautiful white car, and was happy at that moment that I had. So, I sat, nervously but happy to receive him. When he walked out the door with the entourage, I noticed another car pulled up behind me, but as I was in the front, he came to my car first. I said to him, "I want to drive you." He stopped, looked in the back seat and mumbled something about "luggage in my backseat". And then walked away and entered the car behind me.

I was devastated. How could he just walk away from me! I began to cry uncontrollably, but/and as the cars were immediately pulling away, I knew I needed to follow as I did not know where his house was. And through my tears, I took off after the last one. The ski lodge and surrounding properties, which we rented every year in the summer was only so large, and most of the rental houses and condos were within a three-minute drive from the hall. When I reached his house, he was standing outside with a few devotees, mostly young Indian men possibly from Silicon Valley. I got out of my car, still crying from his rejection and walked towards him. When he saw me crying, as did everyone else, he reached out with his arms and let me fall into him. He held me in his arms for quite a few moments, comforting me; which it did. He had never done that before. After some moments, he went inside, and I attempted to follow him, feeling that since he had held me in front of all of them, I would be allowed in. But, as always, they turned me away and told me to come back the next day.

The next morning I drove directly to his house and dropped all of my kitchen supplies off to whoever answered the door and told them, that it was for the guru. And, they took them in. Later that day, I somehow got to ride in the car with him from an afternoon Satsang to his house. We got out of the car and together walked the dirt road going up towards the entrance. It was nice to just walk shoulder to shoulder with him; I hadn't seen him really since Jakarta and it was good to just be walking with him. I told him about all of my purchases in India and that I wanted to cook his meals for him; well of course I was still so insecure, I asked him. And I waited excitedly for his response. He the man of few words turned towards me and shook his head from side to side. Again my heart dropped, I was floored. It was as if the earth opened up and swallowed all of the hope, excitement and joy that I had held since I had bought the pots in India and gotten my nerve and love up to finally take my place with him and was rejected. In hindsight, a simple "Why not?" would have been appropriate. However, I was unable, I think, to ever feel that I truly deserved him; instead I turned and walked away. I walked away dead and lost, filled with disappointment, lifeless. I went back to my cabin and once again cried, cried like I had done, day after day after day. I cried so much that I didn't even know that there was anything wrong with crying constantly. It had become my life; absolute longing and absolute lack of fulfillment.

I did not want to stay at the course, and so I went to the teachers in charge, the same woman who had escorted him out of the birthday event in Jakarta, and told her that I was going to leave and that I wanted my money back. She said they would send it to me. I informed her that I had paid in cash that same day, and she replied that they had already made the bank deposits for the day. The cruelty of the organization was that they never paid me back.

Regardless, I stopped by his house, picked up my pots, got in my car and drove the eight- hour trip back to Los Angeles. The entire way, I felt his energy pulling me back. Desiring me, asking me to return. But I was filled with hurt. Once back in L.A. the energies and the internal requests continued at an intensified level. He was so hard to resist internally. And knowing that I might not see him for yet another three to six months, as he was always traveling, by the third day, I gave in and made the drive back.

When I arrived, he was having a meeting with about forty people. I walked in and he lovingly acknowledged me. I took a seat near the door and happened to notice that his sister was sitting not far from me. One by one, he let people come up to him and talk. When he called me up, she very consciously, stood up and walked out the door. I went to him, and he asked me what I wanted to say, I lovingly shared how much I missed him and cared for him, and he just let me reveal my soul to him in front of everyone.

He asked me where I was staying and I told him I had taken a motel room not far away, he told me to go and rest and come to Satsang that night. I went to the hotel and vibrationally, he poured his love on me in full force. That night when I returned, after Satsang he was seeing a somewhat larger group again in that same room. I was still filled to the brim with the pleasures of the afternoon, and went up close to his seat. I sat there looking at him with complete love and longing and when I got close enough, I whispered in his ear that I wanted him to come back with me. His eyes lit up with a look of surprise, but at that exact moment, his long-time teacher, the woman who had found me in his bedroom in Kaui, stepped through the entire crowd of seated devotees and walked right in between the two of us and said something to him in his ear. He then looked at me and told me to go back to my place and retire for the night.

Oh, if I had only been enough of a woman to tell her to get back!

Much later, when talking to new Indian friends did I see and learn, that when an Indian, shakes his or her head from side to side, it is their way of saying "YES." Almost the opposite head gesture that we use in America. And so, that sideways response to my request to cook his meals had in fact been an acceptance. Oh, how my heart sank upon learning this. He had in fact, wanted me. There was just so much I just didn't understand.

Chapter Twenty-Four
First Lady of the Ashram

The following month, I was so thankful to be back at the Montreal ashram for yet a third visit. The Indian ashram had represented too much pain, as did the German ashram. But Montreal, the home of my soul birth, where I had performed miraculous healings, the place where at least sometimes I was allowed in his home, where I had cleaned his house, where he had cooked for me, felt much more like home. I went immediately to his house, and was thank god, allowed in. The house was full of people as usual, but it was primarily Indians, from India, and not "ashramites" (nickname for those who lived at the ashram in India and were always dressed in white, often looking as if they were attempting to imitate the guru), but just regular middle age Indians, mostly women and a few men, none of whom had I seen before. Not the usual scene of western devotees in his home. It guessed that they had traveled with him from India.

I sat down waiting for him to descend the spiral staircase, watching the group who all seemed to be quite busy, with little tasks. Eventually, in the midst of it all, he came down. I was so happy to see him and he, me. He walked to me, greeted me and we chatted for awhile. He asked me how I had been and how my daughter was. As there were a few others waiting to see him, he went around and spoke to a few people for a couple of minutes. He then asked everyone to leave and go to their rooms and rest. He told me I could stay. As people left, and I didn't, the woman who was the relatively new head of the ashram, who had been my neighbor in Germany, asked me to leave. I didn't move. She then went to the guru to complain about my staying, he took her aside and told her something like "it was okay", but she was not happy and left in a huff. I walked over to him and asked him if there was something that I could do for him. He told me that there were a few dirty clothes on the bed in the back room that I could wash for him and then with most of the people gone, he went back up the stairs.

Remaining were only myself and two other ladies. One of them approached me, kindly asking why I was still there, and I told her that the guru had asked me to wash some of his clothes. She paused thinking for awhile and replied, "Funny I did his laundry earlier today and there was nothing left to be washed." I thought, and I think we both may have thought, "Perhaps he saved something just for me to do......"

The woman and I talked for awhile and we had a very lovely connection, getting to know one another. I stayed most of the afternoon finishing his laundry even after everyone had left the house. As long as one had an assignment, all was well. He left with the group, but I was aware of the unusualness of their visit. That night at Satsang, I got there early in order to get my seat up front center and sat down next to the same woman who I had spoken with at his house. As Satsang was about to begin and the room had filled up, another of the women from the group came towards the aisle, even though we were packed in front, this lady sitting next to me motioned her to join, and squeezed over so that she could fit in, front center.

When the guru arrived on stage, I became quite aware that this woman who came in late was sitting there making suggestively alluring eye movements and gestures towards him. I was not happy that I had allowed her to squeeze in. The nerve of her and the nerve of the other woman to let her act as if she should be up front directly in front with him! Humph! However, once Satsang began, and the guru closed his eyes and went into meditation, and I closed mine, as always we went into Samadhi together, the shakti entered my body and I began to be moved by the divine vibrations. When we both opened our eyes simultaneously, I noticed this woman looking enviously, as no matter how she starred at him; there was nothing that she could do to match the energetic connection between him and me.

One night at Satsang, we all had taken our seats as usual; I was relatively close to the guru, some four rows from the front and a little off to the right side of the stage. But close enough to be near him. I happened to notice two pears sitting on the table next to his seat, which seemed unusual, but often people left stuffed animals and hearts by his seat as gifts, and I guess I assumed these to be personal gifts of fruit for him. When he entered the meditation hall and took hi seat, instead of going immediately into meditation as he normally did, he simply sat in his chair and began to gaze at the entire audience of over three hundred. He slowly and intentionally looked deeply at almost each person. He was in no hurry and must have spent at least twenty minutes just looking and, drawing us in.

Finally, he turned toward the side table, looked first and then picked up one of the pears and ever so gently, placed it on his lap. Then he turned and picked up the second pear, and put it next to the other pear sitting in his lap. And slowly, but without hesitation, he lifted his eyes and turned and looked directly downward and stared straight into my eyes with the most intense love that I could ever imagine, for at least ten minutes. I was absolutely stunned by his gaze. He then went on and held Satsang, but afterwards I could barely move. When I did get up and go to his house, many people were standing in the foyer praying to enter his home. I noticed a well-dressed Indian man who I had not seen before, but who was definitely looking at me, as I at first just waited with all the others. But then, remembering the extraordinary experience only an hour earlier, I went to the door and knocked, and yet once again, denied.

The next day while in the kitchen, someone called me "The First Lady of The Ashram." During that same trip, I was also doing miraculous energy healings with people, so much so that a man came up to me and said that the trees were singing my name.

Chapter Twenty-Five
Yoga in His House

The course continued on with ebbs and tides of frustrations and excitements. I stayed more centered in myself and just allowed things to occur and wished inside that I could spend more time with him. One morning, internally stating this wish and that I would love before I left to actually do my yoga in his house, there was a beautiful peacefulness present and I allowed myself to open to this longing. I got up early and walked over toward his home, perhaps it was 7am. I got there and it was absolutely quiet, no one around, and I knew he did not get up and get going for some time. But the energy guided me to the outer door of his closed-in gazebo entry way. I opened the door and walked inside and thought," I'll just do it here." This is good enough. I am in his space and I am happy. But, just as I was about to roll out my yoga mat, the energy pulled me towards his front door. It reached my hand out and grabbed the handle and turned it. To my great surprise it was unlocked, and I walked in.

There was no one present, and the peace that I had felt outside in no way compared to the absolute tranquility of his home. Energetically, I had always felt that his house felt like my own internal peaceful energy, which many had commented on. Quietly, my body was moved to the center of the room, my mat was laid out, and the divine postures began to flow through me. I was in awe as my body effortlessly, heavenly moved through the asanas with ease and grace.

For almost an hour I flowed slowly and deeply, until on its own, my body rested into a beautiful deep meditation.

As my breath settled, I heard a sound from the back room and I opened my eyes to see two Indian women enter the room. They were surprised to see me, as well and were disturbed and asked me how I got into the house. I responded that I came in through the front door. They told me that I should leave. But I did not move. They looked annoyed and began their cleaning but immediately before they could say another word to me, he descended. They immediately went to him and whispered something about me and he came over and asked me how did I get in, and I replied, "the front door was open." He said "ok" and left it alone. I could tell the women were annoyed, but continued at that point preparing for his morning puja. I was not aware that someone came to do this every day. I just sat still in meditation, and they really began to say that I should leave as it was time for it to begin and he said, "it's okay, she can stay." And unhappily they began to perform the puja and the arti.

Being directly with him, in the midst of this divine ceremony was one of the holiest moments of my existence. Seated directly beneath his feet, only a few inches and being in that sacred space, I was completely out of my body, in the deepest state of consciousness, completely merged into his being. And, as the puja was nearing its end, my head bowed down to the ground and then slowly, inch by inch, it rose pulling my shakti from my crown, up through his feet, through his legs, through his thighs, up his torso, through his heart into his face and through his crown. Shiva and Shakti as one. I was taken aback by the power of this intimate moment as I allowed the vibrations to pour on and on and on. We stayed in this heavenly beauty for as long as we could and were at one. At the end, he told me to go and rest in his guest room and I did.

Chapter Twenty-Six
A Garland of Love

I was feeling very happy and hopeful during those next few months. He had been more welcoming and had opened himself to me in a way that he hadn't in a long time, and of course, constantly expressing his love internally in every way. I was absolutely in love. I had rented a short-term apartment from someone who had taken the course with me, and who happened to be from Israel and was going there for the summer months. One of the head teachers, the man who had been cruel to me in Germany and other occasions was going to Israel to try to open up that country. For the organization's sake, I connected him with this woman who had many contacts, and it did help open up AOL in Israel; however, there were so many complaints about his arrogance and rudeness. I of course ended up regretting making the introduction and over extending myself to someone who had always been so mean to me, organization or not.

My beloved was coming to Los Angeles in the next few weeks, and during our internal conversations, I asked him if this time, he would stay with me and my daughter, instead of at the woman's house where he always stayed when he came to L.A. I was so happy and in love and anxiously awaiting his arrival, like never before. The most important reason was because I had decided that I had had enough confusion about head nods, and what was acceptable to say to an Indian and all of the cultural differences, and now that my daughter had graduated from high school and had a job, I had decided to move to India. I wanted to learn his language, become acculturated and pray that these were the differences, which had kept us apart. Also, India was my home, and had been since that first trip. So again, I asked my daughter if she would please come with me, but told her that I had to move there, she said, "No Mom, don't worry, please go and I will be fine, I just don't want to go there." And so, in addition to simply feeling so at home inside myself in regards to him, I also was happy to ask him/tell him of my decision.

The days leading up to his arrival were filled with bliss. Somewhere along the way I had had someone teach me how to make a garland; what type of string and needle, how to string it, and where and how to thread it through the flowers. And this week, I had decided that I was making one for him, with my own hands; releasing my normal artistic expression fears, and just deciding to just go for it. It was so joyful to go to the local flower shops in Hollywood and take my time selecting the flowers. I decided on deep red velvet roses, purposely to express the depths of my love. I worked on it all day, intricately threading and with each pull, pouring my love into it; until it was filled with the vibration of my heart.

That night, he was arriving at the airport. It was one of the few times that I had gotten the information on his arrival, and with a large group stood anxiously awaiting his coming. All of the women, including myself were dressed our most alluring, one woman attempted to stand out by not wearing Indian style clothing, but wearing a tight fitted Chinese dress. We were all doing our best to get his attention. Like a young girl, with my lei /garland in hand I anxiously stood waiting for him to appear through the gate. And then he came. Radiant, beautiful, everything we each wanted. I was further down the line, which had formed on either side. As he passed each person, a number of people greeted him with garlands, beautiful yellow ones and white ones. By the time he got to me, he was quite full. But, he walked up to me, bent his head down and I, with all of my love, placed it over his head. We then turned and walked off together speaking lovingly. After a few more steps, he turned to his opposite side, where a male devotee who had flown in with him was standing, paused and took all of the other garlands off, handed them to him to hold, and left only mine on as we continued walking. I loved him so.

When we arrived outside by the curb, there was a car already waiting for him, and as I had driven alone, I couldn't jump in. And so we were separated. The evening Satsang was to begin in less than a half an hour, and so I went to my car and drove directly to the event. By the time I arrived, the venue was already packed - over 500 people - and so I didn't even attempt to move up front. I just stayed in the back, and watched from afar. I felt so comfortable and so much love, I didn't mind. After awhile, I turned to my side and noticed a tall handsome Indian gentleman who I had seen once before at the Montreal Ashram, the night where the guru strongly poured his love on me in front of everyone. He was looking at me with great intrigue obviously remembering, almost as much as he was looking at the stage. I simply acknowledged him but turned my attention back to *the* man.

When Satsang ended, I picked up my pace only a little, still lingering in the stillness I felt inside. I did not even try to rush to catch up with him, as I knew that I would join him at the house afterwards. As I walked through the huge crowd, I noticed a beautiful young woman who I knew slightly, gleaming; but mostly I noticed her because she was wearing the rose garland. I greeted her and asked about the garland, and she replied, "yes, the guru gave it to me", gushing with love and joy. I replied, "I know, I made it for him." And she sighed and responded, "Oh my goodness, that makes it even *more* special. I feel sooo honored." I smiled in gratitude and my heart was deeply touched by her words, as I had no idea that she or anyone even knew that he and I were so deeply connected. All the years, loving him so, not seeing or feeling that I was ever externally acknowledged, but here this beautiful angel had so sweetly spoken my truth.

I went to my car and drove on to the house. Somehow I even got a little lost, and I never got lost in my homeland of Southern California, but it took me some extra time. By the time I arrived, he was already locked away in his room, I tried to get in, but no one would let me. I noticed some luggage in the foyer, but I didn't think much of it. While waiting, I turned around and there standing next to me was the same Indian man from the event. He began talking to me about life and work, I told him I had traveled to India a few times and was thinking about taking a teaching position there. He was beginning to share his work with me when we were interrupted by the President of the organization, who swept him away. Later I found out that he was a very important and wealthy businessman who was thinking of investing in an ashram for the Los Angeles area. I was sure they didn't want him getting to know me too much.

Soon I moved out of the foyer and closer to the guru's door when I overheard the owner of the house talking to another woman about how he refused to have his luggage put away. It was very unusual. It didn't occur to me, that perhaps he did not let them put his luggage in his room, because he may have been expecting me to take him away with me....... Eventually, he did come forth and walked directly over to me as I was standing in the center of the living room. There were about 50 people in the house and all eyes were on us. We began to chat, I told him how much I had missed him, and how much I missed India. I shared with him that my daughter was okay and settled and that I wanted to move to India. He looked at me and smiled a beautiful, deep and sincere smile, took a candy out of his pocket, placed it in the palm of my hand and said, "Good!" And that was that.

The next part of my journey was about to begin, I had no idea how it would turn out, but I knew that I could no longer live it the way that I had these past few years. I was moving to India.

to be continued.... ***Autobiography of a Yogini Book II - The Goddess.***

ABOUT THE AUTHOR

Kamala Easton, Ph.D. creator of Embodying the Goddess, Embodying Spirit: Journey towards Enlightenment and Divine Intervention for Weight Management Workshops is a spiritual teacher and a modern day mystic. A life-changing awakening in 1998 transformed Kamala from her academic world, including a Ph.D. in education from UCLA and a B.A. in psychology from UC Berkeley and 20 years in higher education into the realization of her oneness with the Divine.

Kamala has traveled extensively in relation to her teaching and healing abilities throughout India, Canada, Germany, and the United States. She lived and taught off and on in India over a nine-year period. Kamala practiced energy healing for many years, appearing on PBS, Discovery Channel and KCET Los Angeles, and was a member of UCLA Medical Center's Complementary Medicine Pediatric Pain Program. She is also an acclaimed motivational speaker in both education and spirituality and is a certified yoga teacher.

Through her unique down to earth wisdom and humor Kamala imparts the highest knowledge of what is keeping us both collectively and individually from stepping through the veil. Since her transformation, she has been assisting others in their own ascension through sharing her deep love of the Divine, love of self and through letting go of dogma as to how and what enlightenment is.

Autobiography of a Yogini: A Black Woman's Love Affair with her Guru is Kamala's first published book.

Kamala Easton currently lives in Santa Fe, New Mexico where she gives Teaching and Intuitive Readings online and in person.

APPENDIX

REGISTER FOR AN INTUITIVE READING WITH DR. EASTON OR AN ONLINE VIA SKYPE OR PHONE CLASS:

Spiritual Intuitive Reading (1/2 Hr and 1 Hr)
Kamala is a mystic, teacher and intuitive reader who brings information from that place where all is known. She shares the deepest issues of the heart and assists in clearing longstanding problems as well as the deeper understandings of what's to come.

Readings include: relationships, business, finances, health, weight management and spiritual transformation.

"I know it's important to listen and follow our own intuition, but there are moments when we need help. Working with Kamala for me was in the right moment at the right time! Her advice during the session gave me the courage to accomplish the next step of my life and now I just get married!"
Hdk, Espanola, NM

Embodying the Goddess Class (2hrs each)
Kali: Goddess of Transformation
Durga: Warrior Goddess of Protection
Lakshmi: Goddess of Abundance, Beauty, & Bliss
Saraswati: Goddess of Knowledge & Creativity
In India, reverence is given to the Divine Feminine or the Wisdom and Energy of Consciousness. The manifestation of this Divine Shakti or the Powers of the Divine Mother is revealed through various Goddesses. Each workshop includes a discourse on each power or Goddess and through the Body (Yoga), Mind (Chanting the sounds of the power), and Breath (Pranayamas), we begin to open ourselves to these energies.
"I have found Kamala to be an informed and inspired teacher of yogic spirituality, particularly relating to the traditions of the Goddess. She has a unique ability to inspire and to communicate with a diverse audience."
Dr. David Frawley, Director American Institute of Vedic Studies

Embodying Spirit: Journey towards Enlightenment Class (6 Hours)
Join Kamala as she shares knowledge and practices to allow the Spirit of Life to flow through our beings. In these talks, participants will learn to release concepts of enlightenment, which have kept us from true merger. The course consists of Lecture, Intuitive Readings and Meditations. Session Topics: The Possibility of Merging, The Heart, Listening, The Body, The Breath, Knowing, Allowing, Union.

"I attended Kamala's 'Embodying the Spirit' classes via Skype and loved it. She is down to earth and not afraid to laugh at herself. Thank you Kamala for providing me with the insight and tools needed to transform obstacles in my life. I found her support a true gift."
Jen Devi, Missoula, Montana

Divine Intervention for Weight Management Class (6 Hours)
Kamala offers spiritual Insights & answers to the metaphysical causes of weight control. Learn the underlying reasons for our inability to control cravings & identify and maintain a healthy lifestyle. Sessions include: Intuitive guidance, meditations, yoga & chanting to allow for the release of these deep-seated issues.

"The current result? I have lost 20lbs in about 4 months time. I enjoy the feel of my body, the texture of clothes, the person I see looking back at me in the mirror. In finding this healing I have also found my path and am now enrolled in training as a holistic health coach. Most importantly, I recognize myself again."
Dianna White, Albuquerque, NM

Register at **www.embodyingthegoddess.com**

Made in the USA
Charleston, SC
18 July 2014